SOI

BUILDING A REAL ESTATE AGENT'S SPHERE OF INFLUENCE

BRIAN ICENHOWER

Contents

BRIAN ICENHOWER IS THE CEO AND FOUNDER OF ICENHOWER COACHING & CONSULTING (ICC), which provides customized & structured coaching & training programs for real estate agents & team leaders, representing many of the top producing agents in North America. ICC also offers broker/owner consulting on agent recruiting, training & retention. ICC has hundreds of coaching clients and a team of talented coaches. This progressive company also produces online courses, podcasts, training materials, speaking events, video modules and real estate training books.

Brian Icenhower is also the creator of TheRealEstateTrainer.com, the world's leading production training website for real estate agents with hundreds of thousands of subscribers.

Brian Icenhower began his career in real estate as a top producing real estate broker in the early 1990s until launching and operating a number of production-focused real estate offices in California and the Midwestern United States. His implementation of extensive real estate productivity coaching, training and recruiting programs propelled these companies to be repeatedly recognized as some of the highest producing and fastest growing offices in North America by a number of major industry media sources.

Throughout his career, Brian Icenhower has had the privilege of coaching, consulting and training many of the highest producing agents in the country. Mr. Icenhower has also opened various escrow companies, real estate licensing schools, property management and commercial real estate divisions affiliated with these real estate brokerages.

Brian Icenhower is also an attorney, a former instructor in real estate law at the College of the Sequoias, and a frequently published author. Brian served as the President of the Tulare County Association of REALTORS in 2011, and has served as a California Association of REALTORS State Director, a Missouri Association of REALTORS State Director, and as a National Association of REALTORS Director.

ICC OVERVIEW

Icenhower Coaching & Consulting (ICC) provides customized & structured coaching & training programs for real estate agents & team leaders, representing many of the top producing agents in North America. ICC also offers broker/owner consulting on agent recruiting, training & retention. ICC has hundreds of clients coached by a team of talented and experienced coaches. This progressive company is quickly advancing with online courses, podcasts, training materials, speaking events, training workshops, video modules and real estate books.

ICC COACHING & CONSULTING

ICC coaching programs offer much more than just weekly calls with our real estate coaches. ICC coaches are experienced real estate business consultants that offer strategic planning and a full library of training resources to elevate agents' businesses and their careers. Coaching clients are continuously engaged with their coaches through ICC's Online Coaching Platform where agents can communicate with their coach, track their activities, attend training courses, monitor their businesses, and access the ICC training library.

Upon founding ICC, Brian Icenhower inherently understood that people learn and retain information in a number of different ways. Whether it be visually, audibly, verbally, kinetically, or through engaging interaction, ICC's programs are designed to accelerate the learning processes while engaging clients more effectively. Brian set out to create training materials you can print and touch, videos you can watch, calls you can listen to, and workbooks that really break down processes and truly involve agents in the process. ICC's vast resource library is made up of training modules, videos, scripts, tools, job descriptions, budgets, business plans, workflows, systems and other interactive tools to help clients grow their business systematically.

ICC TRAINING MATERIALS

Brian Icenhower's real estate productivity coaching, training and recruiting programs have propelled a number of real estate companies to be repeatedly recognized as some of the highest producing and fastest growing offices in North America by a number of major industry media sources. ICC's production department now produces video training modules on a wide variety of productivity focused topics. These modules come complete with agent workbooks, instructor's manuals and audio files that can be white-label branded for any real estate company. Additionally, ICC's broker/manager coaches are available to consult with company leadership to ensure proper understanding and implementation of brokerage retention, training & recruiting systems.

ICC SPEAKING & TRAINING

Brian Icenhower, along with a number of ICC's trainers and coaches, are available to speak and train on a variety of real estate and business topics by request. Event programs can feature any combination of real estate, educational, motivational, business or leadership focused training as well. Brian's interactive training style provides a high level of energy that keeps attendants engaged and receptive to learning throughout the entire event.

Brian Icenhower has presented for many organizations across a wide number of industries. He has presented at real estate companies, trade conferences, Realtor associations, financial institutions, non-profit & service groups, and for a variety of national corporations. Mr. Icenhower has also been a keynote speaker for numerous organizations. Event sessions can be conducted by the hour, half day, full day or over multiple days depending on the topic and audience. Audience sizes have ranged from a group of ten to a room of thousands.

MODULE 1

Your Book of Business

Sphere of Influence – SOI

Your Book of Business is built on your SOI.

What is an *SOI?* It is your *Sphere of Influence*. Everyone has an SOI. By definition, **your SOI is everyone that you know that knows who you are by name**. That means that you have met them before and they still remember who you are.

As test to determine whether an individual can be considered part of your SOI database, ask yourself the following question:

If someone mentioned me by name to this person, would they recall who I am and state that they knew me or that they had met me before?

If the answer to the question above is "Yes", then this person is qualified to be included in your SOI database. You see that the threshold for admittance is relatively low. Although we will encourage grouping and ranking members of your SOI later on, we initially want to get your SOI referral database set up quickly so that you can start putting it to work right away.

Who Do You Keep Out?

As a rule of thumb:

Your SOI should never include people that you haven't met or who don't recognize you by name.

Continuously staying in contact with members of your SOI database can take precious time and money, so we don't want to waste these efforts on people who don't know who you are. The following are examples of people that do NOT belong in your SOI referral database:

- Inbound internet leads that you have never been in relationship with
- Residents of a neighborhood or community that you have not met
- Members of a company or other organization that you do not know individually
- Buyer or Seller Leads from years ago whom you do not even remember by name

The Watered-Down SOI

A large number of agents with many years of experience will complain about having such large databases that they are unable to utilize them to their potential or do anything with them. These 'watered-down SOIs' are simply too big and unmanageable to work with, and the truly valuable members of these databases are buried within it – possibly lost forever. It's far too cost-prohibitive to send mailers to them all, and there's not enough time to call them all, and so they only get set up on a drip email campaign that results in very little business down the road.

Scrubbing a Watered-Down Database

If you do have a watered-down SOI, the process of **scrubbing** it down to an effectively manageable number is necessary. This process is time consuming but can also be very productive in the short-term as well. Here is how to do it:

1. Scan through your SOI, deleting those you can't remember by name.

2. As you come across names you do remember, contact them right away by phone.

3. Over the phone, ask to update their contact information for your database using our Updating Your Client Database Script

4. Be sure to also ask for business referrals while on the phone with them.

5. Repeat steps 1-4 until your database is scrubbed.

Earn Mind-Share

When it comes to the people you know, how much of their mind-share do you own?

What is *mind-share?* Mind-share means **your name that is the first one on the tip of everyone's tongue at the right moment to send you business.**

- When members of your SOI think of real estate agents, they think of you first.

- Your name immediately comes to mind if they want to see a home for sale or know how much their home is worth.

- If they run into an acquaintance who needs an agent, they are always willing to refer your services.

This is why it is crucial to stay in continuous contact with your SOI: It ensures that you are top-of-mind and thus retain more of their mind-share than any other agent.

Database Contact Plan

What is a *Database Contact Plan?* It is the **systematic process of staying in contact with the members of your SOI.**

An effective Database Contact Plan typically involves making *40 contacts per year with each SOI member.* These contacts are made primarily through email campaigns, mailers and telephone calls. A sample Database Contact Plan might look as follows:

40 Annual Contacts:

- 26 emails (one every 2 weeks)
- 12 mailers (sent once a month)
- 2 phone calls (made once every 6 months)

Why Coca-Cola Still Advertises

This Database Contact Plan of 40 annual contacts allows you to mimic the process of the top name brand consumer products – and our top producing real estate agents systematically copy this tactic, too.

Coca-Cola and those top agents have adopted a Convenience Store Mentality when marketing to their database. This means they are *making it easy to be remembered and found.* Top agents are aiming to be 'on every corner', just like our convenience stores (and Coke), for their SOI members. They are in constant contact and can always be seen by their SOI (and their Coke-drinking customers).

Not only does this keep them top of mind for mind-share, but it makes them very convenient to reach – their contact information comes to each member of the SOI frequently, in a number of formats and media. Whether responding to a Facebook post, replying to an email or calling a phone number on a mailer, top referral agents (and Coke) make it easy to be found. 40 Contacts per year per SOI member and the bottom line results we get from them is why our top agents – and Coca-Cola and other household name brands – continuously stay in touch.

The Real Estate Rollercoaster

The vast majority of agents shut down their marketing department when they get too busy. This creates tremendous gaps in production and income down the road. They start their careers with a lot of income-producing activity to generate a number of clients. Then once agents begin working with clients and handling transactions, they stop actively looking for new business. After all of their transactions close, they panic and start trying to find business again. This cycle can repeat itself for an entire career.

This behavior causes the majority of agents to live paycheck to paycheck, on a constant rollercoaster ride. It's stressful; income is unpredictable; it's hard to pay a business's bills when revenue is up and down. Sooner or later they get tired of riding the rollercoaster and get off. And there are only two ways off. Either they start marketing consistently or close the business, claiming the need for a steady paycheck.

Is Your Marketing Department Open?

Your **Database Contact Plan is your Sales and Marketing Department**. A 'plan' means that you have some system with repeatable and automated aspects to it that make it easy to operate.

Successful businesses understand the importance of having sales and/or marketing departments. Yet many agents claim they don't have enough time to consistently stay in touch with their SOI without sacrificing the level of customer service they provide to their existing clients. Could you imagine other businesses operating this way for very long?

A company with only a customer service department and no consistent sales or marketing operations is ultimately doomed to fail.

This is why it is essential to continuously market to (be in touch with) your SOI according to a systematically applied Database Contact Plan – it ensures that business is always coming in. Business servicing activities can never be an excuse to shut down the marketing department.

Your SOI - The Foundation of Your Marketing Plan

There are many ways to generate business in real estate, but it is well settled that **working an SOI referral database should be central to any real estate agent's lead generation plan.**

Establishing an SOI must be the first step. If done correctly, an SOI should always be the source of most of your business income.

There are many different methods to prospect for business from people that you do not yet know. Many top producing agents are highly skilled at farming neighborhoods, working with For Sale By Owners (FSBOs), contacting expired listings or a variety of other effective business-generation methods. But to prospect for new business without first establishing an SOI database referral system is another quick way to get back on the real estate rollercoaster.

From 100 to 10,000

Agents that don't work an SOI always have to hunt and kill everything they eat each day. They never have any food stored up for the future. Agents with a plan will always outperform (with less stress) those without one:

- A well maintained SOI subject to a Database Contact Plan will continue to yield clients and client referrals over time.

- Agents who maintain a strong SOI frequently receive "come list me" phone calls out of the blue from SOI members that need to sell their house.

- Agent's services are frequently referred from SOI members to other people the agent doesn't even know.

- Agents with strong SOI databases also prospect for new business.

- Agents end up meeting a lot of new people to place in the SOI database.

An agent with 100 people in a well maintained SOI database knows that those 100 SOI members each know 100 more people, and thus the agent's target market is effectively expanded to 10,000 new people. These new people then are placed into the SOI database and increase the amount of referral business received down the road. But without an SOI Database Contact Plan in place, these newly developed leads are typically forgotten and never heard from again.

Nurture & Grow Your SOI

Your SOI is your book of business. Develop it systematically, with focus, and an eye to its key role in the long-term success of your business, as your top priority. Guard it preciously.

As previously mentioned, the implementation of a Database Contact Plan nurtures SOI members and you gain more and more real estate mind-share. Maintaining a consistent focus on growing the size of your SOI is what increases your bottom line year after year.

If developed effectively, it will be your real estate business's most valuable asset. However, the actual net worth of this asset is in direct correlation to how well you nurture and grow it on a continuous basis.

Start by obtaining the names and contact information of the people you know. To do this, we simply ask for the following information:

1. Name
2. Physical Address
3. Email Address
4. Phone Number

We will explore a number of different methods for both nurturing and growing your SOI later on, but for now it's time to get into action.

A well maintained SOI and a Database Contact Plan will continue to yield clients and client referrals over time.

ACTION STEPS:

Start getting in touch with everyone you know, and those who know you by name.

1. Use the SOI Member Contact Form to write down the names and contact information of **at least 20 people** that you know and who know you by name.

2. Make telephone calls to each of the 20 people to update/add to their contact information or ensure that the information you may already have is correct.

3. Ensure that they know, or are at least reminded, that you are in real estate.

4. Lastly, make sure that you always ask them to **refer you to the people** they know. (See points #5 and #6 of the script below).

5. Use the script to below to both grow your database and start nurturing it!

SOI SCRIPT – UPDATE DATABASE

"Hi _____, this is (AGENT NAME) with (REAL ESTATE COMPANY), how are you today?

"I'm calling because I'm updating my customer service database and noticed that I'm missing some contact information like (EMAIL ADDRESSES, PHONE NUMBERS, ETC.) for you. Plus, I need to do a better job of staying in touch with people I know, and I'd love to send you something over the holidays and from time to time. Would that be OK with you?

"Great! So let's see, it looks like I need your (EMAIL ADDRESS) . . . (Obtain any missing information needed for any contact type). Perfect, thank you for your help!

"So is there anything that I can do for you right now? (Respond if applicable).

MODULE 1
ACTION STEPS:

"While I've got you on the line, we are in a hot real estate market right now where homes are selling faster than we can put them up for sale. So, we suddenly have a large number of buyers that we need to find homes for. With that said, do you happen to know of anyone thinking about selling their home within the next year?

"If you can think of anyone, we may even be able to get their home sold without ever going through the expense and hassle of putting the home up on the market. So, if you do run into anyone that's considering selling, would you have any problem referring me to them and letting me know? ... Great!

"Thanks! I appreciate it! Thank you so much for helping me!"

icenhower

One Day – 20 Contacts

Name: _____   Date: _____

	Type*	Name	Ask for Appt?	Appt?	Ask for Referral	Referral?	Follow Up/Notes
1.			☐ Y / ☐ N	☐	☐ Y / ☐ N	☐	
2.			☐ Y / ☐ N	☐	☐ Y / ☐ N	☐	
3.			☐ Y / ☐ N	☐	☐ Y / ☐ N	☐	
4.			☐ Y / ☐ N	☐	☐ Y / ☐ N	☐	
5.			☐ Y / ☐ N	☐	☐ Y / ☐ N	☐	
6.			☐ Y / ☐ N	☐	☐ Y / ☐ N	☐	
7.			☐ Y / ☐ N	☐	☐ Y / ☐ N	☐	
8.			☐ Y / ☐ N	☐	☐ Y / ☐ N	☐	
9.			☐ Y / ☐ N	☐	☐ Y / ☐ N	☐	
10.			☐ Y / ☐ N	☐	☐ Y / ☐ N	☐	
11.			☐ Y / ☐ N	☐	☐ Y / ☐ N	☐	
12.			☐ Y / ☐ N	☐	☐ Y / ☐ N	☐	
13.			☐ Y / ☐ N	☐	☐ Y / ☐ N	☐	
14.			☐ Y / ☐ N	☐	☐ Y / ☐ N	☐	
15.			☐ Y / ☐ N	☐	☐ Y / ☐ N	☐	
16.			☐ Y / ☐ N	☐	☐ Y / ☐ N	☐	
17.			☐ Y / ☐ N	☐	☐ Y / ☐ N	☐	
18.			☐ Y / ☐ N	☐	☐ Y / ☐ N	☐	
19.			☐ Y / ☐ N	☐	☐ Y / ☐ N	☐	
20.			☐ Y / ☐ N	☐	☐ Y / ☐ N	☐	

TOTALS: _____   _____

*Type:
SOI, FSBO, Expired/Cancelled, Circle Prospecting, etc.

Total Contacts Made: _____

Total Appointments Made: _____

MODULE 2 Who Do You Know?

"If I had only stayed in touch with everyone I've known or worked with over the years, I would've had such a profitable SOI book of business by now."

That statement of regret has been made by thousands of experienced agents over the years. Whether you are a newly licensed agent or an experienced agent looking to finally get your marketing department in order, now is the time to get rid of that potential regret forever, so that it never, ever haunts you.

You Are More Popular Than You Think

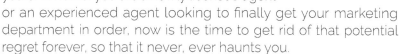

Most people vastly underestimate the number of people they know. Our SOI's threshold is relatively low for admitting people into our general SOI database.

When in doubt, again just ask yourself the following question:

If someone mentioned me by name to this person, would they recall who I am and state that they knew me or that they had met me before?

Think of all of the people that you run into on a daily basis that you already know on some level – even the people that acknowledge you as you walk by, shop at the grocery store, attend your child's school event, or who comment on your Facebook posts. We run into people we know everywhere, even though we can't recall them from memory when put on the spot to do so.

Your SOI is a Living, Breathing Database

Your SOI referral database must continually grow and evolve, just like a human being over his lifetime. Your database must naturally grow as you encounter more and more people. As a matter of course, the number of past clients in your database will increase as you close more real estate transactions. When you meet new people or join new social groups and organizations, your SOI database will evolve right along with you.

But we have to first 'give birth' to our SOI referral database. We need to start somewhere. The key is to purposefully engage our mind and recall as many of the people we already know. This gives our database instant life.

Start with Your Strongest Advocates

Who are 'your' people, your advocates and cheerleaders? The people who are closest to you, of course. The people you know the best. The people that care about you and your success the most. These are your strongest advocates. They want you to succeed and are willing to help you grow your business. They collectively generate the bulk of a newly licensed agent's business. Since they know and trust you, it is easy for them to promote you to the people that they know. Typically, your strongest advocates can be found in the following categories (and by extension, the network of each of these people):

- Friends
- Spouse and immediate family
- Extended family (relatives)
- Past co-workers
- Neighbors

Reaching out to these key people to obtain or update their contact information (physical address, email address & phone number) will give your SOI referral database birth. But don't assume that they will champion your cause without instruction. It is equally important that they are reminded you are in real estate and could use their help. Simply ask:

"Do you know anyone thinking about moving this year?"

When put to your strongest advocates, this question often renders highly productive results. Regardless of their answer, it is equally important to follow up with

"If you do run into someone thinking about moving, can I count on you to recommend me by name and get their phone number for me?"

Understand that the key here is to be vulnerable. These are your supporters. They want to help you succeed, so providing them with instructions for how to do so will be appreciated. This is what 'activates' your database to give it life – so be confident and direct with these questions.

Who Else Do You Know?

As previously mentioned, you know a lot more people than you can recall. So let's start with some places where you might keep large groups of people that already know who you are. Even if all that you have right now is a name, write it down and include it. The key for now is to expand the number of people – **names of people who know your name** – in your SOI referral database. We can fill in the blanks later. Here are some of the more **common locations you store the names of people** that you already know, so go there now and start writing names:

- Mobile phone contacts
- Wedding lists
- Facebook, LinkedIn and other social media 'friends' or 'followers'
- Email contacts
- Neighborhood directories
- Church membership lists
- Social activities directories, including sports team rosters

Then move into the following **categories of people** and do the same. If you are married, be sure to dive into those people your spouse knows in these types of groups, too.

- Local family, relatives
- Friends, acquaintances
- Clubs, organizations
- Sports clubs or gyms, workout groups, team sport players
- Neighbors
- Your children's teachers, coaches, tutors
- Past co-workers
- Professional service providers (doctors, dentists, therapists, attorneys, CPA/accountants, etc.)
- Tradesmen who provide services at your home (painters, plumbers, pool/lawn services, etc.)

Remember not to dump every name from any of these sources into your database unless **you know each of them and they know who you are as well.** The last thing we want to do is water-down your database at its birth.

Your Database Means Business

Believe it or not, there are still many more people you know who belong in your SOI referral database. Use the following list of businesses and service providers to further grow the SOI database of people you know. Carefully read each line and quickly write down the names that come to mind for each category on your SOI Member Contact Form.

Who Do You Know from These Industries?

Accountants

Alarm/Home Security Companies

Appraisers

Appliance Stores

Architects

Asbestos Mitigation

Attorneys (General Practice, Real Estate, Family/Divorce, Wills, Trusts, Estates & Probate)

Auto Body Shops & Repair

Auto/Car Dealerships

Auto Mechanics

Baby-Sitters

Banks (Personal & Business)

Builders (New Home & Improvements/ Add-ons)

Cabinet Supply & Installation

Caterers & Party Planners

Carpenters

Carpet Cleaners

Carpet Supply Stores

Chimney Cleaning

Chiropractors

Cleaning Services

Computer & Networking Servicers

Concrete, Cement & Pavers

Construction Contractors

Countertop Supply & Installation

Credit Unions

Day Care

Deck Construction/ Repair

Dentists

Dermatologists

Doctors

Dry Cleaners

Dry Wall Companies

Electricians

Engineers (Civil & Structural)

Estate Sale Companies

Event & Community Centers

Excavating Services

Fencing Companies

Financial Planners

Fireplace Supply & Repair

Flooring Companies

Florists

Furniture Stores

Garage Door & Repair

Garden & Nurseries

Geological & Soil Testing

Gyms & Fitness Centers

Hair Stylists

Handyman Services

Home Inspectors

Home Stagers

Home Warranties

HVAC Companies (Heating & Cooling)

Insurance (Auto, Health, Homeowners, etc.)

Interior Designers

Jewelry Stores

Landscapers

Lawn Care

Locksmiths

Masonry

Mold Inspection & Mitigation

Mortgage Lenders

Movers (local & national)

Mud-Jacking Companies

Music (DJ & party services)

Nannies

Notaries

Office Machines (copiers & printers)

Office Supply & Furniture Stores

Optometrists

Orthodontists

Painter

Pediatricians

Pedicure Shops

Personal Trainers

Pest Control Companies

Pet Kennels

Pet Sitters

Photographers

Plumbers

Pool Contractors

Pool Care & Supply

Pressure Cleaning

Printing Companies

Property Management

Radon Inspection & Mitigation

Rain Gutter Installation & Repair

Restaurants

Roofing Companies

Senior Living Communities (Convalescent Homes & Assisted Living)

Septic & Sewer Companies

Siding & Stucco Contractors

Sign & Banner Companies

Snow Removal

Spa & Tub Supply/ Service

Sprinkler/Irrigation Supply/Repair

Stock Brokers

Storage Companies

Surveyors

Tax Exchange (1031 Tax Exchange Consultants/ Accommodators)

Tailors

Tile & Grout Contractors

Title & Escrow Companies

Trash Disposal & Hauling Services

Veterinarian

Video Services

Water Damage Remediation

Wedding Planners

Well Inspection & Testing Companies

Window & Glass Supply

Window Covering Supply & Services

Window Cleaning

SOI SCRIPT – UPDATE DATABASE:

"Hi _____, this is (AGENT NAME) with (REAL ESTATE COMPANY), how are you today?

"I'm calling because I'm updating my customer service database and noticed that I'm missing some contact information for you (LIKE EMAIL ADDRESSES, PHONE NUMBERS AND ETC.) Plus, I need to do a better job of staying in touch with people I know, and I'd love to send you something over the holidays and from time to time. Would that be OK with you?

"Great! So let's see, it looks like I need your (EMAIL ADDRESS) … (Obtain all missing information) … Perfect, thank you for your help!

"So is there anything that I can do for you right now? (Respond if applicable).

"While I've got you on the line, I wanted to ask you who you might know that might be looking to move in the near future. Maybe a friend, family member or co-worker? Can you think of anyone right now?

"If you do bump into anyone looking to move, would you have an problem referring them to me?

"Great! Thank you so much for helping me!"

SOCIAL MEDIA SOI DIRECT MESSAGE SCRIPT

"Hi it's (Agent Name). How have you been? I'm updating my real estate database and I'd love to send you something over the holidays and from time to time. My real estate business was amazing last year, but I need to do a better job of staying in touch with people I know. So would you mind replying with your current home address, phone number and email address to help me out? Thank You! "

ACTION STEPS:

1. **Fill out the SOI Member Contact Form** with the names of all the people that you recalled or located in the ways shown in this module.

2. **Call 10 people on your SOI Member Contact Form per day** to update, complete and correct their contact information.

   a. Use the quick script questions:

   "Do you know anyone thinking about moving this year?"

   "If you do run into someone thinking about moving, can I count on you to recommend me by name and get their phone number for me?"

   b. or the full SOI Script – Update Database shown above. Make sure they know you are in real estate and instruct them on how to refer you to the people they know.

3. **Send 10 direct messages per day on social media** channels like Facebook or LinkedIn using the Social Media SOI Direct Message Script at the end of this module.

MODULE 3

Your SOI Contact Plan

The key is to be systematic in contacting all individuals who are in your database. That is where too many of us fail.

Communication with your SOI referral database must be consistent in order to generate predictable results. As we discussed in Module 1, members of your SOI should be **contacted 40 times per year** using a variety of communication tactics, in order for you to have true mind-share – to stay top of mind when it comes to real estate. This continuous contact with your SOI database ensures that your marketing department always stays open by generating a steady flow of leads.

Your Plan for Making Contact

We have a diversified Plan of Contact which all SOI members benefit from. They are primarily among three media, which comprises the core of your approach:

1. **Emails**
2. **Mailers**
3. **Phone calls**

However, SOI Contact Plans might also include:

1. **Drop-by visits**
2. **Face-to-face visits**
3. **Facebook and other social media messages**
4. **Client appreciation events**
5. **Delivery of hand-written notes**

Focus on the frequency. The key here is **quantity not quality.** Avoid contact methods that involve too much time or expense. Frequency of contact, rather than the amount of impact that any individual contacts may make, is what we aim for.

Keeping in mind the Convenience Store Mentality explained in Module 1, we diversify the contacts through different channels to ensure that we are always 'on every corner'. Plus, varying the media of communication with SOI members to all eight of these ways prevents us from appearing overly aggressive or intrusive with any one particular contact method.

Like a Bouquet of Roses

Think of preparing your SOI Contact Plan as if you were assembling a bouquet of roses for a loved one. Of course, you focus on roses, but you would likely also include a vase, some water, a card, and maybe some greenery or smaller flowers to accent the roses, and even perhaps a little instruction card stating how best to make the roses last longer. Likewise, the florist wants your loved one to know where you shopped, so the floral business has its logo, name and contact information on a gift card, too.

Similarly, the combination of telephone calls, emails, mailers, visits and so on helps round out your Contact Plan's effectiveness. Each method of contact plays a part in the overall delivery of your marketing plan.

CRM for Mind-Share

If your SOI Contact Plan is like a bouquet of roses, then think of a CRM as your florist.

What is a 'CRM'? It stands for 'Customer Relationship Management', and today usually refers also to a software system that helps agents

- Assemble and store member information
- Arrange members by action, type or category that you select
- Manage and even pre-schedule communications broadcasts and media involved (such as email or phone call)
- Follow up with members in a timely manner

Most real estate CRMs provide agents with attractive email and mailing templates arranged into **campaigns** that the system will send out (or 'broadcast') automatically on behalf of agents. These CRMs also will keep track of the daily telephone calls agents need to make order to keep up with their SOI contact plans. CRMs are extremely useful for template designs, automating contacts and keeping contacts organized. There are more functions of interest, but all CRMs offer these basics. A CRM is used with the goal of improving business relationships and developing mind-share in your SOI.

This said, using a CRM is not an absolute necessity. Most free email services provide features that allow you to store and arrange contacts on their platforms as well. Even long before the existence of the internet, many successful agents managed to organize and stay in continuous contact with their sometimes quite large databases by utilizing folders, day-planners or even rolodexes to organize contact information. The tools are numerous; the choice is yours.

Whatever tool you select, make sure to use it systematically.

Now let's examine some of the different SOI Contact Plan components that help us assemble and arrange your bouquet.

Emails – The Baby's Breath

Emails are used primarily to gain mind-share, not to collect business.

Just set it and forget it. The good news about email campaigns is that they typically cost no money and require a minimal amount of time to set up and manage.

After being written and scheduled, they send the messages automatically without further intervention. Emails can be sent by your CRM to SOI members automatically over the course of a year.

Note, however, that **emails have a relatively low lead generation rate** when compared to the other means of communication in your SOI Contact Plan. Although an SOI Contact Plan composed of 40 emails a year may seem both inexpensive and efficient, it is also relatively ineffective.

As a rule, **no more than 26 of the 40 contacts in your SOI Contact Plan should be emails**.

To help you understand this rule, think of the small white flowers called Baby's Breath frequently included in bouquets of roses. A bouquet of just Baby's Breath doesn't have anywhere near the same impact as a bouquet that also contains roses. The Baby's Breath accentuates the roses to give a greater overall effect. Think of emails as the Baby's Breath of your SOI Contact Plan. They should never be used as the only way of connecting with your SOI.

Emails in summary
      Pros: Inexpensive and take little of your time.
      Cons: Highly ineffective used alone.
      Rule: No more than 26 of the 40 contacts in your SOI
             Contact Plan should be emails.

Mailers – The Vase

Mailers are those printed materials that arrive in your mailbox. If emails are the Baby's Breath of your SOI Contact Plan bouquet, then think of mailers as the bouquet's vase.

Mailing materials are tangible and can even last a while. They can sit on countertops or be placed on refrigerators with magnets. If nothing else, mailers are usually held for a while and viewed at least once before being thrown away. This makes them more impactful than emails.

Most real estate CRMs also contain pre-made mailing templates for agents. Some CRMs even contract directly with a mailing service to send mailers to your entire database throughout the year, automatically. So as with emails, sending physical mailers to members of your SOI takes very little of your time once they are set up.

Here's the catch though: Mailers cost money. The cost is typically anywhere from $0.75-$1.25 per mailer for both printing and postage. Price generally depends on the number of mailers and the quality of printing.

As a rule, **the cost of mailers can never exceed 5% of your GCI** (Gross Commission Income).

Since we also recommend that any agent's **marketing costs never exceed 10% of GCI**, mailings to SOI members should be regarded as a real estate agent's most significant cost of doing business. *In fact, we recommend that first-year agents with no history of commission income limit their marketing costs solely to SOI mailers.*

> Mailers in summary:
> **Pros:** Take little time and are more impactful than emails.
> **Cons:** They cost money.
> **Rule:** The cost of mailers must not exceed 5% of your GCI.

Telephone Calls – The Roses

Phone calls are the roses in your bouquet. If roses draw the eye, phone calls draw the recipient's attention, too. An SOI Contact Plan without phone calls is like a vase filled with only Baby's Breath and no roses.

The vast majority of your referral leads will come from these calls, so it is important to systematically make them in a continuous fashion. It is also important to mention that telephone calls cost you absolutely no money.

As rule, **your contact plan must contain at least 2 phone calls to each member of your SOI.**

This said, these roses do have some thorns. The downside is that telephone calls are where most agents fail in keeping up with their SOI Contact Plans. Many use no scripts and flounder once they have an individual on the line. Others plead 'no time'.

Agents fail here, but there is really no reason to do so. It is a matter of math, and calling consistency. If you have 250 people in your SOI database and you plan on making 2 telephone calls to each of them as a part of your Contact Plan, you can expect to make a total of 500 phone calls per year. If we only plan on making calls during week days (Monday – Friday), there are approximately 250 total business days each year to make these calls. Thus, *we only need to make two calls per day* to keep up with our SOI Contact Plan.

500 calls ÷ 250 days = 2 calls per day

Two calls per day doesn't sound too bad, especially put in the context of the total number of calls you make and receive daily.

Telephone calls in summary:

Pros: They generate the most leads; they cost no money.

Cons: You must make them yourself and it's easy to get behind on your calls, or flounder if you don't have a script.

Rule: Your contact plan must contain at least 2 phone calls to each member of your SOI.

Other Types of Contacts

Although we strongly recommend keeping it simple during your first year or two managing an SOI Contact Plan, there are other contact methods that you can include in your plan as well.

- Direct **engagement on social media** networks like Facebook can be fast, easy and effective.

- In person **drop-by visits** to deliver pies at Thanksgiving or maybe pumpkins at Halloween can make a huge impact, even though they are very time consuming.

- **Client appreciation events** can draw a large number of your SOI right to you.

- **Handwritten notes** can provide a very personal touch from time to time.

The list of different ways to contact SOI members can go on forever, so we will address many of these methods in more detail in later modules.

Sample Database Contact Plans

Before you start creating your own database contact plan, we have provided you with the following sample plans to give you an idea of some different options that may best serve your specific needs.

Remember that all your contacts must add up to

40 total contacts per year per member.

Also make sure to keep in mind the previously mentioned SOI Contact Plan rules:

- No more than 26 of the 40 contacts in your SOI Contact Plan can be emails

- The cost of mailers must not exceed 5% of your GCI

- Your contact plan must contain at least 2 phone calls to each member of your SOI per year

Sample Plan No. 1 – The Basic

There are no awards for style points. Automating both emails and mailers in a CRM campaign by using a CRM's ready-made templates is our recommendation for getting into action quickly. You connect with each member of your SOI database over the year through:

- 26 emails
- 12 mailers
- 2 telephone calls

Sample Plan No. 2 – Giving to Get

Although this SOI Contact Plan is both pricey and labor intensive, it's designed to get big results. By continuing to provide something of value throughout the year, SOI members are more likely to be appreciative and willing to provide referral business. We recommend this plan only be used on smaller SOI databases or just those SOI members that you count on the most.

- 18 Emails – Automated in CRM to send every 3 weeks
- 12 Mailers – Sent monthly as follows:
  - January – "Happy New Year - Thank you for making it a great year" postcard with photo of team
  - February – flyers/coupons for local area home, garden & patio show
  - March – local college & pro sports schedules
  - April – local & national market update
  - May – flower & garden seed packets
  - June – summer local events update: graduations, water park coupons, summer camps, etc.
  - July – local & national mid-year market update
  - August – back to school shopping coupons & sales
  - September – flyers/coupons for local area home, garden & patio show

- October – local & national market update

- November – canned food drive (leave bags on doorstep to pick up) & include holiday recipe

- December – Happy Holidays cards

- 3 phone calls

- 1 Drop-By – pumpkins delivered to doorsteps (October/November)

- 1 client appreciation event – tailgate & skybox at pro sports event

- 4 Invitations to client appreciation event: 2 emails, 1 mailer and 1 phone call

- 1 Post-event email showing photos of event highlights & announcing event contest winners

Sample Plan No. 3

This cost-effective plan puts less emphasis on mailers and more on agent activities like phone calls, Facebook direct messages, drop-by visits and inexpensive items of value.

- 4 quarterly newsletters – mailed out every 3 months

- 26 Emails – automated in CRM and sent every 2 weeks

- 1 client appreciation event – held at an open house in December: photos with Santa

- 4 Invitations to client appreciation event: 2 emails, 1 Facebook direct message and 2 phone calls

- 3 phone calls to SOI

- 1 Facebook direct message - to update Database Contact info

- 1 drop-by visit to deliver single bag of microwave popcorn with business card – "just popping by"

Use the following page to create the first draft of your own SOI Contact Plan. Review some of the ideas contained in the 3 sample contact plans shown above.

Remember that your total number of contacts must add up to 40 per year per member, and don't forget to follow the three rules below:

1. No more than **26 of the 40 contacts** in your SOI Contact Plan can be emails

2. The cost of mailers must not exceed **5%** of your GCI

3. Your contact plan must contain at least **2 phone calls** to each member of your SOI

My SOI Contact Plan [write out your plan here]

MODULE 4

What's Your Number?

Real Estate Listing

THIS IS A LEGALLY BINDING CONTRACT BETWEEN A LICENSED REAL ESTATE BROKER AND YOU. THIS FORM HAS IMPORTANT LEGAL CONSEQUENCES AND ALL PARTIES SHOULD CONSULT WITH AN ATTORNEY IF NOT UNDERSTOOD COMPLETELY. THERE ARE DIFFERENT TYPES OF BROKERAGE RELATIONSHIPS WHICH INCLUDE BUYER AGENCY, SELLER AGENCY AND TRANSACTION BROKERAGE.

All else being equal, you can often determine the success of a real estate agent by the size of his or her database. As we have discussed, birthing and staying in continuous contact with your SOI is crucial. Systematic communication with your SOI through a Contact Plan is only part of your focus. It is equally important to make continuous efforts over the life of your business to grow your SOI database as well.

Always remember that **real estate is a game of touches**, so the more people that agents can build relationships with directly correlates to the amount of business they conduct. The size of your database matters, and being intimately familiar with the number of people in your SOI is crucial. Have your calculators handy because it's time for some math!

Tennis Anyone?

Before playing a game of tennis, most tennis players warm up before a match by hitting tennis balls back and forth to each other before officially starting the match and keeping score. During this warm up period they don't exude much effort. They don't hit the ball with much purpose or put much pace on their shots. Players still warming up won't chase too hard after their opponent's shots either since they aren't too concerned about the outcome.

Yet the degree of effort changes significantly the minute that they decide to start keeping score. Suddenly the players care. They focus on strategically placing each of their shots; they strain to catch up with balls that land in odd corners of their court. This is because the players are now concerned about the outcome of their efforts. Having a scoreboard matters. Keeping score motivates these athletes to put more effort into their actions, which in turn creates better results. This type of focus also makes the game more fun.

The same can be said about the management and growth of your SOI Referral Database. Agents that just contact SOI members when they feel like it simply don't get the same results as top producers who keep a daily scorecard. Too many excuses get in the way, and whether it's poor time management or simply caving in to a 'don't feel like it' mood, agents without preset objectives for contacting and growing their databases can't compete with those who do. When your business success and household income are on the line, your performance becomes a lot more important than a tennis match.

Don't Play Without a Scoreboard

You cannot do business with people who don't have a connection with you. The SOI – that database which gets fuller and fuller of names of people who know your name and that you are a real estate professional – is your real business.

Agents who fail to set and hold themselves accountable to goals for contacting and growing their SOI database soon find their marketing departments shutting down completely. They hop on the real estate rollercoaster by focusing solely on customer service, yet soon find there is no one left to service. They frequently don't find motivation to start conducting income producing activities again until their production drops to a dangerously low level. This up-and-down pattern can repeat itself so many times that agents will start to accept this volatility as just the 'nature of the business'. Without established expectations that hold you accountable to contacting and growing your SOI Referral Database, they may just be right.

Agents who just take whatever business naturally comes their way through casual relationship building, and doing only what feels natural to them, often operate with a sense of uncertainty about where their next commission check will come from. They start to believe that business is hard to come by, that it is a game of luck. **A scarcity mindset takes over**. The fear of losing clients is stronger than their desire to do what it takes to generate more business. This mindset causes them to forget what their business generation plan even is, and they flounder.

The Numbers Don't Lie

The National Association of REALTORS® produces annual membership statistics that reveal some astonishing facts:

- 33% of newly licensed agents quit real estate after their first year
- 87% of agents leave the business within their first 5 years
- 89% of all transactions are handled by only 11% of agents in the United States

Hopefully these numbers don't scare you. Instead they should motivate you. Understand that the single reason that such a large majority of agents leave the business is because they don't make enough income, and they don't make enough because 1) they never learned how or 2) they don't practice what they actually have learned. It is crucial to consistently focus on business generation activities and never let customer service demands be the excuse for shutting down your marketing department.

These numbers should also clearly illustrate that only a shockingly small percentage of real estate agents consistently attempt to generate business at all. That means that there is very little competition for agents who protect their business generation time, track and increase their number of touches, keep their eye daily on all their marketing efforts and always know their numbers. In turn, this business oriented mindset creates predictable results that allow the agent to thrive and prosper over the long term in the industry.

Agents who know their numbers and work their Contact Plan come from an abundance mindset.

They operate with a sense of confidence and security because they know that their activities create predictable results – and an abundance of commissions.

Lucky Number 7

It's lucky for you that your SOI Contact Plan creates very predictable results that you can rely on. Based upon decades of coaching, training and tracking the results of real estate agents, we know that for every 7 people in your SOI database with whom you make 40 annual contacts, you can expect to close 1 transaction. This conversion ratio is so important that it bears highlighting:

The completion of an SOI Contact Plan with *40 annual contacts* will result in *1 closed transaction* for *every 7 people* in your SOI Referral Database.

Since the mathematical wheels in your head are already turning, let's jump right into the math. Apply this **7:1 annual conversion ratio** to a hypothetical agent's SOI Referral Database of 300 people. This is also a good time to reiterate the criteria for SOI Referral Database membership: If someone mentioned our hypothetical agent by name to these 300 SOI members, all of these people would recall who the agent is and be able to state that they knew him or that they had at least met him before. So now let's do the math:

- 300 SOI Referral Database members receive 40 annual contacts, resulting in 12,000 total touches per year for your business, most of which are automated

- Applying our 7:1 annual conversion ratio, 300 ÷ 7 = 42.86 (rounded up to 43)
- That's **43 closed transactions** in a year from this SOI Referral Database alone!

For new agents, you may cut these numbers in half for your first year, when you have followed the birthing process for your SOI database, collected complete contact information from each of those 150 people, prepared and set up the contacts (emails, mailers, etc.) and automated them. That is still over 20 closed transactions from a 'starter' database!

Hitting the Commission Jackpot

To drill down on these results even further, let's assume that the average home price in our hypothetical agent's area is $250,000. If he charges an average commission of 3% per transaction side, he will **earn $7,500 in gross commission income (GCI) per closed transaction.** If he closes the 43 transactions from his SOI Referral Database as shown above, the math is simple:

- 43 Transactions x $7,500 GCI = **$322,500 in annual gross commission income**

Does this business revenue seem too good to be true? It shouldn't, not if you go back and re-read the above real estate industry statistics – and remember that the vast majority of agents simply don't put forth the effort or make the time to keep their marketing departments open long enough to make 40 diversified contacts to their SOI a year. Most don't even make the time to gather the contact information of the people they know, and organize them in one place. Agents are often unwilling to embrace the technology associated with creating email campaigns, pay the costs associated with mailers, or put forth the effort to make daily telephone calls. **All you have to do is be the 1 agent out of 100 that actually does it!**

How Does Your SOI Measure Up?

Now it's your turn. It's time to determine the types of results you can expect from your own SOI referral database. Use a calculator to complete the steps below and establish the predictable results that you can expect from the successful completion of your SOI Contact Plan.

1. Refer back to Module 2 to help you estimate the number of people in your SOI Referral Database. Fill in approximate numbers for each of the **Module 2 categories** below:

   - **Strongest Advocates:** Close friends, immediate family, relatives, past co-workers & neighbors.

     - Number of People: _____

   - **Places You Keep Groups of People You Know:** Phone contacts, wedding list, Facebook friends, church membership lists, neighborhood directories, sports rosters, etc.

     - Number of People: _____

   - **All the People You Can Remember in Your Major Sphere Categories:** Family/relatives, friends/acquaintances, clubs/organizations, sports teams/gym workout, neighborhood, school teachers/other students, professional services providers, etc.

     - Number of People: _____

   - **Business and Service Providers You Know:** Refer to the list of business industries in Module 2 to inspire you.

     - Number of People: _____

2. Add up the 4 totals in #1:

   - Total number of people in your SOI Referral Database: _____

3. Divide the total number of people in your SOI Referral Database by 7 to determine the number of transactions you can expect to close per year, after making 40 diversified contacts on these people according to your SOI Contact Plan.

- Total Number in SOI _____ ÷ 7 = _____ Annual Transactions Closed

4. In order to determine the annual gross commission income (GCI) that you can expect to receive from your SOI Contact Plan, you need to know a few numbers that are specific to your business and local area. Fill in the blanks below.

    - \$_____ = **Average Home Sale Price**. Use the average home price in your local area.

    - _____% = **Commission Percentage.** The average commission rate you charge per transaction side when representing either a seller or a buyer. If you don't know, use 3%.

    - _____ = **Annual Number of Transactions Closed.** The number of annual transactions closed from your SOI Contact Plan. Use your total from #3.

5. Using the three figures that you put in the blanks in #4, calculate the annual gross commission income you can expect to earn from the successful completion of your SOI Contact Plan:

    - Your GCI per transaction: Average Home Sale Price \$_____ x Commission %____ = \$_____

    - Annual Number of Transactions Closed _____ x GCI per Transaction \$_____ =

    - \$_____ = Your Annual Gross Commission Income from you SOI Contact Plan

Don't Postpone Your Rewards

It's essential not to procrastinate on making your 40 annual contacts. Picking up the phone requires no more preparation than grabbing your printed script, pen and paper. Start making your first round of telephone contacts to each member of your SOI Referral Database right away.

Don't wait until you have all of your email messages written and loaded into the auto-responder or all the various mailers' content created and planned before reaching out; get your first one or two emails and mailers written and set up (automated and scheduled to send immediately). Send the first ones out right away, so that you don't leave potential business on the table. As they go out, you are writing the next email messages and scheduling them, and so on, until you have a complete set of messages that require very little maintenance.

In other words, don't simply *prepare* to generate business, start right away! Start generating business and leads even as you are getting your SOI Contact Plan created and organized.

SOI SCRIPT – UPDATE DATABASE & ASK FOR REFERRAL

Hi _____, this is (AGENT NAME) with (REAL ESTATE COMPANY), how are you today?

I'm calling because I'm updating my customer service database and noticed that I'm missing some contact information for you (LIKE EMAIL ADDRESSES, PHONE NUMBERS AND ETC.) Plus, I need to do a better job of staying in touch with people I know, and I'd love to send you something over the holidays and from time to time. Would that be OK with you?

Great! So let's see, it looks like I need your (MAILING ADDRESS) ... Thanks! How about your (EMAIL ADDRESS - OBTAIN ANY OTHER MISSING INFORMATION) ... Perfect, thank you for your help!

So is there anything that I can do for you right now? (RESPOND IF APPLICABLE).

While I've got you on the line, I wanted to ask you who you might know that might be looking to move in the near future. Maybe a friend, family member or co-worker? Can you think of anyone right now?

If you do bump into anyone looking to move, would you have a problem referring them to me? Great! Thank you so much for helping me!

1. Set up your email and mailing campaigns for your SOI Contact Plan.

   a) Acquire a Customer Relationship Management (CRM) **software package**, or decide on another long-term system you can depend on.

   b) Either **use the pre-made templates** provided by your CRM software system or start creating the content for your first few emails and mailers yourself as described in this module.

   c) It is essential to **send out your initial emails immediately.**

   d) **Send out your first mailer right away.**

   e) **Keep writing and setting up** email messages and mailer content (scheduling them for broadcast to your SOI database as they become ready) until you have a full set prepared.

2. **Continue making your first round of telephone calls to all the members of your SOI Referral Database** – update their contact information while also asking for referral business. Use the scripts previously provided in Modules 1 & 2 or try out the script above.

Feeding the machine – the marketing machine for your business – is all about creating growth.

It should now be easy to see why most top producing real estate agents get the bulk of their business from their SOI Referral Databases. It's a reliable and predictable machine that pumps out big numbers at a 7-to-1 ratio – as long as it is regularly maintained at 40 diversified contacts per year per member.

No matter what business the entrepreneur is in, he needs to build a marketing machine.

However, most top producing agents aren't satisfied with simply maintaining their production and income levels. That is, as we saw in Module 4, you may develop 300 members in your SOI Referral Database. And, it is true, the 7-to-1 closing ratio may hold true with those 300 members year after year for several years for you.

However, your business is not really growing. It is doing essentially the same number of closed transactions every year. Even if that income is great, a healthy company is a company that's growing.

Since the SOI Referral Database is the foundation of an agent's marketing plan, that means that you need to increase the number of members of your SOI database and do it every year. For that, you need to go beyond 'who you know', which is how you birthed your SOI database. You need to meet 'new faces'.

SOI Referrals versus Prospecting

As we've shown, staying in contact with the people in your database via an SOI Contact Plan is extremely lucrative when done consistently. There are numerous ways to prospect for business from people you don't yet know as well, and you need to use them fairly soon in your business. To attract those 'new faces' and make them SOI members, you go prospecting. What is 'prospecting'? It is contacting people you have no prior connection to and interesting them in your real estate services. Another common name for prospecting is 'cold calling' or 'cold contacting'.

You first establish an SOI Referral Database of the people you already know and who know your name as the foundation of your marketing plans. Then, once you begin to prospect to people you don't yet know, you initiate many new relationships; these new faces are immediately added to your SOI Referral Databases and added to the Contact Plan. This way you are assured to have mind-share of the new people you meet, and prevent those relationships from fading away into forgetfulness.

Agents must repeatedly ask for referrals from members of their SOI database as well as prospect for new business (and then ask those new faces for referrals) – but without an SOI Contact Plan running on their SOI database, they are spinning their wheels. They constantly have to look for new clients because they hold little hope of business coming to them from existing and past relationships. We will look at a way to prospect in Module 6 that is highly effective, and not really about 'cold' calling/contacting as is most traditional prospecting.

Goals for Expansion

Just like setting a goal to contact 10 people in your SOI Referral Database per day, it is equally important to set goals around the growth rate of your database. We hear of some setting goals for 'measured' or 'slow' growth – that simply means they decide in advance what number of new SOI members per year is 'easily achievable' for them and take actions to achieve those numbers.

For agents in their first year of building a database, they will likely remember and run into many people that they already know throughout the year that aren't yet in their SOI databases. Think about all of the people you haven't seen in a year or so that you run into at the grocery store, the gym, your child's school event, the coffee shop, or anywhere you're out and about. This happens to most people year after year, and thus these 'new faces' are added to the SOI database as they are encountered.

Therefore, it's not an unrealistic goal to add 5 people to your SOI Referral Database per week every year. Let's see how those numbers work out. With a total of 52 weeks in a year and 2 weeks off for vacation, you have a total of 50 working weeks in a year. 50 weeks multiplied by 5 people added per week adds up to 250 new people for your SOI Referral Database, each having 40 contacts per year. Here's a quick summary of that math:

- 50 weeks x 5 new faces = 250 people added to SOI Referral Database.

Now we can apply our 7-to-1 SOI contact plan conversion ratio to these 250 people that will be added to your SOI. Thus, we divide these 250 people by 7 to predict an additional 36 transactions (35.7) closed the year following their membership in your database.

- 250 people added to SOI ÷ 7 = 36 additional transactions closed the following year

It starts to get easy to see how top producing agents rapidly increase their production each year. As with the example we used in Module 4, an agent who has an existing SOI Referral Database of 300 people can expect to close 43 transactions (300 ÷ 7 = 43) per year.

If we incorporate our current example, we will add another 36 transactions the following year to bring next year's total to 79 closed transactions (43 + 36 = 79).

- Year 1 - 300 People in SOI ÷ 7 = 43 transactions closed in year 2
- Year 2 - 250 Peopled added to SOI ÷ 7 = 36 additional transactions closed in year 3
- Year 3 - 550 People in SOI ÷ 7 = 79 total transactions closed in year 3
- The story gets even more compelling if we look at additional commissions earned.

Assume that the average home price in our agent's area is $250,000. If he charges an average commission of 3% per transaction side, he will earn $7,500 in gross commission income (GCI) per transaction closed. Then the math works out as follows:

- Year 2 - 43 transactions closed x $7,500 GCI = $322,500 in annual GCI
- Year 3 - 79 transactions closed x $7,500 GCI = $592,500 in annual GCI

NOTE: Don't expect to receive a 7-to-1 conversion ratio from your SOI in the same year people are added to your SOI. There is a one-year lag time, since it takes 40 diversified contacts over the period of a year to your SOI before you can expect these results. Agents should anticipate these returns in the year after SOI members are added or in the members' second year in your database. Every member you add to your SOI database is building your business for next year and the years thereafter. All the more reason to start growing the SOI right away.

Spend Money to Make Money

The growth of your SOI Referral Database contributes directly to the growth of your business and your income. Suddenly it's a lot easier to comprehend some basic business expenses in a fuller context. This 'measured growth' is why successful agents are willing to spend what seems like a lot of money (at least initially) on mailers andCustomer Relationship Management (CRM) systems.

Even paying a $40,000 annual salary for a full-time administrative assistant starts to seem very inexpensive. The time and (initial) discomfort associated with making daily telephone calls to your SOI start to seem well worth it, too. Indeed, as the number of closed transactions swells and your bottom line increases, those expenditures suddenly seem minimal.

Yet frequently these expenses seem so far out of proportion to immediate returns on that money invested that they prevent the vast majority of agents from building their SOI, launching their Contact Plan, and achieving such phenomenal results. It's entirely up to you to decide if you will let these concerns stand in your way or if you will trust the process and find a way to overcome them as they arise.

Growth over the Years

Assume that we use similar figures for average sales price ($250,000) and commission charged (3%) as we did above. The following chart illustrates the predictable results agents can expect from such sustained SOI Referral Database growth each year:

Number of People in SOI	Transactions Closed	Gross Commission Income
300	43	$322,500
400	57	$427,500
500	71	$532,500
600	86	$645,000
700	100	$750,000

We assume a steady 100 new faces per year entering your SOI database. This is only 2 new members per week!

Activities Create Results

Now that you've seen the potential results, it's essential to commit yourself to the activities that drive them. Top agents that run successful SOI based businesses understand the importance of both contacting their SOI 40 times per year and growing their databases consistently with new faces. Remember that your 'basic' Contact Plan includes emails, mailers and phone calls. Contacts made by email and mailers are automated and typically go out through an agent's CRM. That just leaves telephone calls to complete the 40 annual contacts in an agent's basic SOI Contact Plan.

As previously stated, it's not uncommon for a top producer to set an expectation to call 10 SOI members per weekday while also adding 5 new members to his or her SOI database per week. Although these preset and measured objectives may be simple (anyone can do them), understand that they are certainly not easy (not everyone has the raw determination and focus to carry it off).

Simple ≠ Easy

Protect Your Marketing Department

There are far too many obstacles that can stand in the way. Otherwise everyone would be achieving the amazing results shown in the SOI Database Growth Chart above. Don't take your Contact Plan lightly or cut corners at any time. Be aware that once you start generating active clients and closing transactions, the customer service mindset will try to consume you – you will be tempted to take care of current transactional business and forget, first for one day, then a week or month, to do the business- and SOI-building work we have been describing. Customer service work ensures a good reputation for your business. But marketing work expands it.

You might already suspect where the discipline comes in, where excellent time management plays a huge role.

Once you start generating clients, you will start to feel as though you don't have time to make your 10 daily phone calls to your SOI.

And you'll need the time, too. Calling people you already know takes some time, because people in your SOI will naturally want to do a little catching up when you call, and talk for a while.

You should anticipate every 5 SOI telephone contacts you make to take 1 hour.

5 calls - 1 hour

That means it will take 2 hours to talk to 10 members of your SOI per day without interruption. To play it safe, if you try to limit each SOI conversation to 10 minutes, you should have 10 minutes to spare (5 contacts x 10 minutes = 50 minutes) in each 60-minute hour.

Also understand that a 'contact' means that you have a live conversation with each person. *A contact is not*:

- · an attempted-dial with no answer
- · a text message
- · leaving them a voice message

A 'contact' is a true conversation, where you talk live to ask especially about their real estate needs, update any missing contact information and also ask for referral business ... as well as chat a bit to catch up and build the relationship.

Conducting these conversations in an uninterrupted manner while you have active listings, pending transactions, daily commitments and a myriad of other intrusions is no asy task.

Scheduling, time-blocking, accountability, preparation and systems are all required to ensure that these marketing activities are accomplished and recorded each day.

We will address these essential disciplines in future training modules, but for now let's start taking some concrete action.

SOI SCRIPT: ASKING FOR REFERRALS

1. "Hi _____, this is (Agent Name) at (Real Estate Company), how have you been? This is a quick call about business. I'm reaching out to remind you that I'm in real estate! You see, statistics show that our clients are going to run into 6 to 10 people over the next 12 months that are looking buy or sell a home. So can I ask you a favor?"

   (If yes . . .)

2. "I prefer to grow my business by word of mouth. So when you bump into these people, would you be willing to refer my services and call me with their contact information?"

   (Pause and wait patiently for a response. Let silence do the heavy lifting here)

3. "Thank you for thinking about it for me! Oh, and since I've got you on the phone, do you happen to know anyone that is thinking about buying or selling a home right now?"

4. "Thank you for taking the time to think about that. I'll be in touch!"

NOTE: A follow up "Thank You" card can have a very positive impact.

1. **Add 5 new people to your SOI Referral Database per week.** Be sure to get all of their contact information up front since you now know how hard it is to reach back out to them to obtain any missing information.

2. Continue making your first round of telephone calls to all the members of your SOI Referral Database to update their contact information while also asking for referral business. **Make 10 SOI telephone contacts per day.** Use your scripts. Ask for referrals in each and every conversation.

"If you don't receive enough, have a look if you give enough."

—Jennifer White

You now understand the importance of systematically contacting the people in your SOI referral database while you continuously grow the size of your SOI at the same time. **These two poles of focus are the foundation of your marketing plan that cultivate and grow your book of business.** As a result, top producing agents consistently conduct activities that accomplish both of these objectives simultaneously.

In Module 5 we mentioned prospecting for new faces to grow our SOI, and here we'll examine one of the most effective strategies for doing so.

Real Estate Referral Networks

No one refers more clients to other businesses than real estate agents, so top agents understand the importance of capitalizing on this power by **developing real estate referral networks.**

What is a 'network'? It is a group of businesses, associations or individuals with one or more shared interests. When you enter or belong to a network, there is no cold calling or contacting, since you have one or more shared interests with all members of the targeted network.

As a real estate professional, you will find shared interests in many types of networks in which you can profitably and easily prospect, or network. Your goal is to turn them into a 'referral machine' for your business.

Whether it is businesses closely affiliated to real estate like mortgage lenders, title companies and home contractors, or businesses or professionals in other associated industries like civil engineering, law, accounting, real estate lending and investing, architecture, property development – agents with strong real estate referral networks know how to accumulate an army of professionals all working to refer clients to them.

You want to build partnerships. As the name implies, it is not a one-way but two-way street. Give and take is vital, and your focus will beneficially be more on *giving*. A two-way relationship allows you to refer your clients to these other businesses and professionals, even as they refer business to you.

Let's examine the systems, methods and scripts agents use to build powerful referral partnerships.

Business to Business Marketing

What is *'business-to-business marketing'* (or B2B marketing) for your real estate activity? It is you – a business – approaching other business owners or representatives to ask for referrals. Some prefer to avoid the word 'marketing' and just call it 'networking' (or in our case, 'referral networking'). Whatever you call it, you need to do it to grow your SOI.

Since clients frequently look to REALTORS® for suggestions on everything from local child daycare providers to a reputable plumber to interior design specialists, it's essential to consistently and purposefully instruct business referral recipients to also send clients back in return.

This said, agents don't need to refer business before initiating a referral relationship with another professional. Simply contacting business owners about the idea of developing a referral partnership in advance of having any actual clients to refer to them is the preferred method for generating immediate business while also growing your SOI referral database quickly. Doing this form of business-to-business marketing with consistency slowly builds an army of professional advocates looking to drive home buyers and sellers your way in the hopes of being paid back with your client referrals in the future. It is a back-and-forth sharing between you and the other business.

Provide value or make a contribution before expecting anything to come your way.

Come from Contribution

If you are hesitant to ask business owners to send clients your way, first understand that you must do so in a way that provides value to them by **coming from a place of contribution.** For example, you may cringe when yet another home inspector calls you to use his services. However, if the primary purpose of the inspector's call was to refer you a listing, then your attitude towards the conversation might change dramatically. When approaching these incoming (they call you) or outgoing (you call them) conversations, embrace the mindset that you have future business to provide these prospective partners. You are always **giving to get business.** Come from an attitude that you have a lot to give.

These are very positive conversations that will usually be received very warmly, from one businessperson to another. Most business owners are very agreeable when other people commit to increasing their business income. They will have no problem returning the favor. Think about how you would feel if the tables were turned. What if a mortgage broker called and told you that she has clients that she prequalifies to buy new homes that also need an agent to list their existing homes for sale? A phone call like this would make an agent's day. As loyal as you may feel towards your current lender, you would be likely to send home buyers to this new referral source in hopes of getting more listings in return.

Before continuing to read, flip ahead to the scripts at the end of this module to get a feel for the content of the conversations you will be having when you reach out to cultivate business referral partnerships. As you can see, these are easy contacts to make because you are giving other people something they want: More business. Additionally, not only are you agreeing to refer clients to these professionals, you are also agreeing to market on their behalf as well.

Enhancing the B2B Referral Relationship

There are a number of ways agents can add further value to their business referral partnerships that will increase the number of client referrals they receive.

Many agents will hold **vendor appreciation events** where all of their referral partners are invited to a party, happy hour, sporting event, luncheon or other types of social gatherings. Many agents will even have their closely affiliated vendors sponsor these events to cover the event costs. However, agents will often receive enough referrals at the actual event itself to easily cover its expenses a few times over. Plus, these service providers will be provided the opportunity to network with others to further expand their own spheres of influence.

As you develop your partnerships, you need to keep a written list of the services and trades your referral partners offer, and make sure your own clients get the list. Agents with established referral networks frequently provide prospective clients with such a written **Preferred Vendors** list featuring all of the professionals from various industries that they recommend. This vendors list promotes the agent's professional partnerships while also providing a convenient service to his or her real estate clients. Many agents will feature their preferred vendor list on their **agent website** as well. This web page typically provides vendor contact information and can even feature links to each vendor's website. Many agents also provide clients with a **mobile app** that features a preferred vendor list as quick reference for their clients.

It's also common to reach an agreement with vendors to **offer special promotions to an agent's clientele**. For example, agent Annie Thompson's clients might be instructed to ask for the "10% Annie Thompson Discount." Not only does this provide value to Annie's own clients through a money-savings opportunity not available elsewhere, but it also drives business to Annie's referral network as well.

Preferred vendors are also more likely to refer clients to agents who regularly **promote their businesses on social media.** Regular promotional Facebook posts that include photos of their business or product with a link to their Facebook page can go a long way to remind referral partners that you are continuously working for them and that they need to refer business to you.

Create Your Referral Network Vendor List

Use the sample vendor list below to help you think of professionals and businesses to contact and create new referral network partnerships – then start building your own list. Also remember that it is advisable to **establish partnerships with more than one provider for each industry type** since you never know which will start to actively refer business to you in the future until it actually happens. It's better to have a number of fishing lines in the water if the goal is to catch more fish. Once you start receiving business from certain vendors (and this can unfold over one, three or more years), you can send them referrals back and start pruning your list down to only those that actively participate in the referral partnership.

SCRIPT NO. 1 – REFERRAL BUSINESS PARTNERSHIP

Hi (business owner), I'm John Smith with ABC Realty and I'm in the process of creating a list of preferred business & service providers to give to my clients and include on my real estate website. Since I frequently have clients ask me for a good (profession), I'm looking for a trusted professional/company to refer them to. I've heard good things about your company, would you and your business be interested in being included?

Great! I like to establish these professional referral partnerships to help grow each other's businesses as well. So if I were to refer clients to you, would you be willing to refer your clients that are looking to buy or sell a home to me with the assurance that I will provide them with the high level of customer service that you expect?

Excellent! How about we exchange each other's contact information so that we can get started?

SCRIPT – FOLLOW-UP AFTER REFERRING A CLIENT TO A VENDOR

Hi (business owner), I'm John Smith with ABC Realty and I just gave your contact information to some clients of mine that need (service/product). Would it be OK if I gave you their contact information so that you can reach out to them as well?

I'd also like to continue to refer clients your way in the future too. In fact, I am in the process of contacting various businesses that I can refer to my clients and include on a list of preferred business & service providers to give to them. I would also include this list on my real estate website. Would you be interested in being included?

Great! I'm looking to develop these professional referral partnerships to help grow each other's businesses, so if I continue to refer clients to you, would you be willing to refer your clients & friends that are looking to buy or sell a home to me?

Excellent! So it looks like you already owe me one! I'm not kidding, you had better get on it so that I have to keep sending business your way in return! Does this sound like a good plan to you?

SCRIPT NO. 2 – REFERRAL BUSINESS PARTNERSHIP

Hi, this is John Smith with ABC Realty, and I was making a list of the best businesses, services and products in the area for all our new customers and your business (company/practice) came to mind. I was calling to see if you were accepting new customers and if it would be OK if I referred clients to you?

And what would be the best way to refer your business? Email, phone or your website?

The only thing I ask is that if you get a customer that I referred could you just let me know so that I know my efforts have been working?

Since I have you on the phone, do you have two people that you refer real estate related business and questions to?

Much like you, I am always looking to build new relationships and find new customers as well. If I am someone that you would feel comfortable referring business to, I would propose that we work together to generate business.

You might be impressed by all the marketing that our company does and how that could help your business as well. Maybe we could talk later in person or on the phone about some joint marketing ideas?

SCRIPT – TO CONTACT SOI TO GROW VENDOR LIST

Hi _____, this is John Smith with ABC Realty, and I am reaching out to you for a recommendation. I am attempting to enhance the customer service that I provide by expanding the list of trusted professionals and business vendors that I recommend to my clients. So whether it is a financial planner, auto mechanic, or anyone that has done work around your home, who do you know that did a great job for you that I could recommend more business to? (Continue to prompt them for trades/professionals you know you are looking for, too)

Thank you! Would you mind if I mentioned that you referred me when I reach out to them?

Great! One last question, if you were to run into anyone looking to buy or sell real estate would you be willing to refer them to me?

That's great! Thank you. And before I let you go, you don't happen to know anyone thinking about buying or selling their home in the next year do you?

1. **Add 5 new Business Referral Partnerships per wee**k to your SOI Referral Database. Add them to your CRM as such, or use the SOI Member Contact Form.

2. Make **10 telephone contacts per day** to potential Business Referral Partners and/or SOI members by using the following scripts. This sounds like a lot? Remember you are actively and consistently asking for referrals during these calls, as well as building relationships.

3. **Create your own Preferred Vendors List** from the above activities to provide to your clients in the future. Remember that this a continuously evolving document that you should always be adding and deleting from over time. Get it started now with the few vendors you have and watch it grow as you establish new referral partnerships.

MODULE 7 — Search Updates

The SOI Database and your (basic or advanced) SOI Contact Plan is the foundation of your business-building marketing strategy. As for any business we want to grow, we need to be able to market to new and more people month after month. This module will show you **how to utilize auto-prospecting search update tools** to consistently add value and come from contribution, to both grow your SOI but also to consistently contact members of your SOI over time.

As we are aware, to grow a sphere of influence, or SOI Referral Database effectively, we must make a consistent effort to both grow the number of contacts and to contact the members of our SOI. By utilizing an **auto-prospecting search update tool**, we can do both at once.

For example, to **grow our SOI**, we must meet new people. As we meet those people, we need to stay in touch with them, build rapport with them, and do that by adding value – from their perspective. Whether prospective clients are looking to buy

ic

or sell a home or even just stay up to date on the value of their existing home, we can do that by giving them information about the types of homes they are looking for, the current value of their own home, or the values of surrounding homes over time. So, if we use a search update tool to systematically stay in contact with them by keeping them up to date and informed in this way, we can make continuous contacts and build rapport. We get to the point where we will ultimately come to know them and be able to add them to our sphere of influence database.

Similarly, we can **stay in contact** with our existing database by offering this very same information to current members of our SOI. Utilizing search update tools can clearly be used to 1) add value to and build rapport with people not in our database and 2) stay in contact with existing members of our SOI over time.

Continuously growing, cultivating, and staying in contact with your SOI is **a game of touches.** The more touches you can make, the better off you are. However, it gets increasingly difficult to make a large amount of contacts with the same people without annoying them or turning them off. Because of this risk, we want to make sure that we come from contribution to them (adding or bringing value), especially if that value can be very relevant to real estate and home values.

MLS Searches Versus Websites

There are a few ways real estate agents might set individuals up on a search where they will have access to all the homes listed in a local association of realtor's multiple listing service, or MLS.

Most MLS platforms provide a free tool for all realtor members to use allowing them to input the name, property address,and contact information of a client. It can also set them up on a search with specific search criteria for homes, whether it be geographic location, neighborhood, size of homes, price of homes, certain amenities, and so on. In this way, the prospective client will receive an automated email every time a home comes up for sale that fits his specific criteria. This is a free service that most all multiple listing services provide to their realtor members.

However, many agents opt to purchase an individual website and customer relationship management software tool, or CRM, that provides a similar feature through an IDX feed with the local multiple listing service. It feeds the data for all the same houses through the website and CRM system to individuals that a real estate agent sets up on a similar home search auto-drip email campaign.

Advantages of the Website

The **first benefit** to the agent that purchases this website CRM system is that as all the emails go out to prospective clients that are set up on this search. Many of these prospective clients will click on the links in the emails to view the homes shown. When they click on these links repeatedly, they visit the agent's website and oftentimes browse on them. As these prospective clients are clicking on the agent's website, suddenly search engines like Google and Yahoo take notice.

As the various search engines take notice of all the traffic that's hitting these sites, the search engines then start to rank the websites higher, and the website becomes more visible, which serves to attract more leads and more potential clients and consumers to the agent's website. Many agents opt to use their own website just to be able to drive more traffic to it through the email auto-drip campaign. These websites can cost anywhere from $100 to $1,500 a month depending on the amenities, features, etc. However, agents may still opt to utilize the free service provided by the multiple listing service as well.

A second advantage for purchasing and paying for your own website is that there is oftentimes artificial intelligence, or AI, behind the site that will alert the agent when specific clients are visiting the site. This provides information about how long they looked at different homes, how long they stayed on the site, which homes got the most traffic, etc. This AI often comes in the form of text and email notifications to the agent, so the agent is immediately alerted – even while the prospective client is actively searching on the agent's website. This can be an advantage: agents know they have the highest rate of contact with a prospective client when that client is actively looking on a website at homes. This is your highest conversion rate for contacting clients. When they happen to be in the mood to look at homes is the easiest time for a realtor to make contact.

If an agent delays contacting a client until later when the client is no longer actively looking for homes, they may be playing with kids, on the way to the store, taking the trash out – all times they don't want to answer the phone. If they do happen to answer the phone, it's received as a nuisance call and they respond by saying that they're busy. Their mindset is not focused on looking for homes. But if the agent can respond immediately while they're on the site searching, that mindset will be very much geared and interested in receiving help, information, or support about the homes they're looking at. That's what they're current focus is on, and you are supporting that focus and answering those questions. So, an agent calling then is going to be more welcomed than when they are doing something else. That website – and following what it is doing – can help you.

A third reason that agents will use a website is detail. Because the website search features are a little bit more detailed, a little bit more customized to the agent, look a little bit more professional than the standard one presented by the multiple listing service, you benefit from more data. Although the multiple listing service website is very effective, it brands all the listing and emails as if they are coming solely from the agent that is sending them. Even though homes may be for sale by many other agents that are members of the local multiple listing service, all the listings of all the homes that are sent to prospective clients via these emails will appear as if they are listed by the actual agent that set the search drip up. No other agents will be contained in those emails – you will be the prospects' contact focus. This is not the case with the website through the IDX feed to the MLS.

Multiple Uses of the Search Update Tool

We can use the search update tool for **four** general areas.

First, we can use it **to stay in contact with** our **sphere of influence,** by keeping contacts up to date and adding value. Add value either for their current home by sharing how its value is changing, or on the comparison sales in their existing neighborhood, since we know that homes are valued and priced based in comparison to others nearby of the same type, called comps. We can keep our SOI up to date on their own neighborhood and their own home.

Second, we use it to **keep agents up to date, in specific geographic farms**. A geographic farm will refer to specific communities, areas, or neighborhoods that we are marketing to consistently and systematically that comprise our target market. Often, you'll see agents do this with things like, American flags on the 4th of July, Christmas cards, market update fliers, mass mailings, fliers, door hangers, cold calls to the neighborhood. We can also keep members of that neighborhood up to date on their values from the privacy of their home by setting them up on neighborhood home search tools for the entire neighborhood's sales activity.

Third, we can use it for **seller leads**. Prospective home sellers thinking about moving within the next two years may not even be members of our SOI. They may be people we meet that are thinking about selling in two years whom we set up on a home search for their home and neighborhood, so that they can stay up to date on how the value of their home is changing, what the sales activity is like, how quickly homes are selling in their neighborhood. When it comes time for them to move and they want to sell their home, they'll be educated as to what the homes are worth, how quickly they sell, and what their competition will look like based upon the other homes that are actively for sale nearby. It may help them dictate when they're going to move. They may not be wanting to move until they can get a certain price for their home. Watching the pricing of homes sold in their neighborhood might help them decide when to move – if we keep them up to date. All the while making this contribution to them will keep you at the top of their mind when it ultimately becomes time for them to sell and buy a new home.

Fourth, buyers. Buyers are a little bit different., this is the most traditional use of a home search tool; agents have been using it for a decade or so. This is where we actually find a buyer wanting to buy a home. We set them up on an automated home search based upon the criteria they have for a new home.

With buyers, we're looking for the home that they want to purchase and base our search on their criteria for maybe an entire city, or those specific neighborhoods in the city they want to move into. Criteria include a price range, or a pool or other certain amenities, a three-car garage, etc. We can really drill down on the specifics they're looking for and only show them homes that come up for sale that meet that specific criteria.

So far, we've been setting home owners as **sellers** to keep them up to date on their local market status and changes. They see other homes that go for sale, go pending and under contract, and then they ultimately sell their home with their own idea of perfect timing. In fact, it's very possible to set up any **potential home seller on two searches: as a home seller and as a home buyer.** Get in the habit of setting up each seller as **both** a buyer and seller.

The four multiple uses of the search update tool are your SOI, geographic farms, seller leads, and buyer leads.

No matter who it is, we need to remember just about everybody we meet will be in one of those four categories. So, any prospective lead, whether it's SOI, farm, buyer, or seller can go on some sort of update neighborhood drip tool so that we are always sending auto emails about either their existing home or the home they're looking to buy. A real estate agent should really focus on putting everyone on at least one of these drips. Every single person they encounter is on a drip, and thus the likelihood that we're going to get more and more business is increased.

For example, if we had 30 members of our SOI on a drip, 50 members in a neighborhood, 15 buyer leads, and 5 seller leads all on drips, we should have a hundred people on email drip campaigns. From that, let's say that we might be able to sell five houses in the next 12 months to those people. Now, imagine if we had 500 people set up on email drips – multiply our sales by five and thus increase the likelihood that we would sell 25 homes. The more we can get set up that we are consistently staying in contact with, that we're consistently adding value and coming from contribution to people, the increased likelihood that we're going to get more sales.

Stop just meeting people and hoping you remember to follow up with them.

Think about building rapport and offering value right away to everyone you meet. Even though they're not ready to buy or sell right now, what this provides is a tool that we use to create and come from contribution and help everyone with something tangible and valuable to them. We help them buy or sell real estate right now. And then from the comfort of their own home, without any pressure or obligation, they can start receiving that value by looking at homes, and can stay in touch constantly, see our name regularly, and constantly know that we're giving them this value ... until they are ready to buy. We are available to them in the next email or in our follow-up phone call to make sure their search is going okay, to help them buy a home. So, everyone goes on your search update tool. Everyone. And the more you get and the more contacts that your emails are making, the better your chances of closing more sales more easily.

Your Neighborhood Auto-Email Drip Script

This auto-email scripting is basically designed to create **a value proposition based on their own neighborhood information** for members of your sphere of influence. It creates a means for you to stay in contact with them, and to have your name at the top of their mind over time, both by email and phone. It gives you a script that's broken down and really adds **six key value proposition points** in the middle of the script. **These value proposition points should roll off an agent's tongue every time we talk to an SOI member** that we want to set up on a search. Because once we can get an SOI member set up on a search, our name can stay top of mind much easier when they think of real estate, because they'll always be receiving emails from us about homes that come up for sale and sell in their current neighborhoods.

And those six emailed propositions are easy:

1. They can look through all the **photos of their neighbors' homes.**

2. They can compare the **amenities, features, and size** of the listings that come up for sale to their own homes.

3. They can know the **price** of each new listing to get a rough idea of the current value of their own home.

4. They can see **how quickly homes sell** and **the final sale prices.**

5. It will give them a good idea of how the **value of their home** is increasing over time.

6. It will keep them up to date on their local **neighborhood market conditions.**

These six points could also be stated quickly in purposeful phone call made to each SOI member. They could also be contained on a postcard, like an invitation to be on the lookout because we set them up on an automated search for their neighborhood as a customer service that we provide to all our clients. So, we can use that script in an introductory email before the searches start, in a mailer, in a digital image like a PNG or JPG that is sent as a personal message, or as a private message on Facebook to every member of their SOI that is a Facebook friend.

Touches are the key here. Remember, **real estate's a game of touches**. We want to make many repeated touches through a variety of communication channels and media. So, whether that's email, direct mail letter or postcard or flyer, a phone call or a Facebook private message, we can introduce this new customer service feature to all our clients through multiple, well-understood, frequently used channels. Creating ways to add additional touches that are done automatically without our even having to do an ounce of work, always with our name, always with our own contact information, containing real estate relevant information that they can engage with and interact with.

On your normal database contact plan for your SOI sphere of influence, **we recommend at a bare minimum that we email, mail, and phone all our members of our SOI 40 times a year.** And oftentimes the real touches that matter are the phone calls, because emails and mailers are often regarded as trash. Although it's important to activate these forms, they have a lower engagement rate than direct phone or face-to-face contact. However, email is something that they look forward to, that they open, that they click to go to your website, and thus is much more powerful than mailers and certainly a standard templated email without personalization. This is a powerful engaging touch that gives them something they want. They want to see what their neighbor's home around the corner is selling for.

Too often, people walk around their neighborhood and see signs go up for sale and never know the price, never know if or how fast it sells. Now, they can click on those homes and go look through photos of their neighbor's home, compare those amenities to their own home, really be up to date on how hot the market is and how fast homes are selling and what prices they're selling for. They can get a rough idea of what the value of their home is over time and they get addicted to looking this up. They come to appreciate the agent because the agent is clearly the one sending this link, this information to them. Their name is all over the email and all over the website, so they know who's giving them this value and who's keeping them up to date.

This is **real-estate-relevant**. This isn't just generic ways to contact people you know. It is not just being top of mind for them because of your gift baskets, American flags, refrigerator magnets and calendars. This is very much helping them with real estate information that is relevant and timely. It reaches them in a way that they want to receive it. We often consider this search setup one of the most powerful touches we make. The automation makes it "once and done" for us. Once we get the search set up and we call them to introduce it, it has a very strong impact.

The hardest part about it is calling each of the members of your SOI to let them know that you have set them up on a search. When we do call them all, we use the script that we have provided for you, the neighborhood auto-email drip script. And we let them all know, and the way that we do that is saying we have already set them up on a search, and we would love their feedback about it. We don't ask permission. We don't ever want to ask permission to send them emails, or people just give a knee-jerk decline response to that. We want to inform them that we've set them up on a search, and we really want their feedback. We can also let them know that we can turn the search off. In other words, they can unsubscribe, or they can reply to it and we'll turn it off, but we'd love their feedback first. We call them to let them know it's coming, and most people will receive it and will like it.

Later on, we talk about ways to use this tool as a means of lead follow-up, so we can constantly stay in touch, not just with the emails, but calling them on the phone as well. But, this provides a great tool for us to move forward, stay in contact, add value with our SOI, and continue to stay in touch and be the real estate agent of choice for every one of our SOI members.

Geographic Farms

Now we share the **geographic farming** auto email drip script. We use this geographic farming auto email drip script for phone and in-person contacts, as well as for email and mailer content.

This is when we present ourselves as the real estate expert for a **local community or neighborhood**. The script is geared towards neighborhood housing information. We create a neighborhood logo, neighborhood or area name. We repeatedly use the **logo and name** for that neighborhood because they're more likely to open emails that are specific to their local geography. Giving their own name to the neighborhood avoids a sense of spam email. If you live in Amber Meadows and you receive an email about Amber Meadows, you're more likely to open it, since it pertains to you and your local community.

These are easy searches to set up. The key here is to get the email addresses from all the people that live in the neighborhood. And this can either be done the old-fashioned way, by just collecting them over time on open house sign-in sheets, by knocking on doors and getting contact information and offering them the script. Or it can be done in a more modern, progressive way, where you can purchase email addresses per geographic location from a variety of database sources online.

Once we have those, then we can use them to create a farm database with each resident's phone number, mailing address, and email address, and we'll want to categorize this group in our database by that neighborhood name. **Note that these would not necessarily be members of our sphere of influence because we don't know all the people in a farm yet.** However, we can still market to them. As we get to know them, they can then become included in our SOI. We can still target and market to them and we can use the script provided as the introductory email. We can send it in a mailer to them, introducing our neighborhood search tool, our neighborhood update tool. We can also call them and let them know as well.

The key is that the script is very similar to our SOI script, with the same six value propositions. We just refer to it as a neighborhood. And it's much easier to set up the searches for the residents of a neighborhood because they're all on the exact same search. With our SOI, we must go in and look at the address of every single SOI member because they live all over a city or area. And we must set them up on neighborhood searches for each neighborhood they all happen to live in.

However, for targeting one geographic neighborhood as our geographic farm, they're all really going to be on the same exact search. So, we can set up the same search for everybody in that neighborhood and market it as our "Amber Meadows Neighborhood Update", and introduce this as our Amber Meadows neighborhood update tool. And it's a customer service that we are providing to all the residents of Amber Meadows to keep them up to date on their neighborhood housing market. And we can use all six value propositions quite easily. It's a great marketing tool to add value, come from contribution, and conduct a lead follow-up over time with members of a geographic farm.

Seller Leads

This is for anyone we meet that's not in our SOI but who might be a prospective lead to sell their home. This automated email drip tool will keep them up-to-date on their neighborhood's home market: the price of their home and those around them; how fast homes on the market are selling and the prices they're selling for; the amenities nearby homes have in them. This allows prospects to compare them to their home, so that they are educated about the price of their home and their neighborhood real estate market when it comes time for them to sell.

The key to this approach is in bold in the opening paragraph of the script, where we say, **"This will help you stay educated about your home's value and your neighborhood's conditions leading up to whenever you are ready to move."**

By keeping them up-to-date systematically with this email drip tool, and by calling them and following up with them from time to time about how well they like the tool and getting their feedback on the tool, you'll be able to build rapport with them and establish a relationship with them. Later you include them in your SOI; this becomes a way to grow our SOI. We meet new people while also setting ourselves up to work with these potential sellers until they list their home for sale with us.

You will use this script a lot, because this is anyone you meet, and you are ready when they say, "Oh, we're thinking about moving, yes, but not for a year or two." Often, real estate agents will not really consider such people a hot lead and they don't put any effort with them and they go off, forgotten. When a seller's that far out, we wrongly ignore them, when we should be coming from value and contribution to get them ready for that sale.

What we're recommending you do is say, "Well, we've actually got something to help you in the meantime. We've got a tool that'll help you stay educated and up-to-date on your housing market," and it offers them and you an effortless way to track and follow up and slowly build rapport with them. This tool adds value through information and education until they are ready to sell. It puts your name out in front of the pack. And often, you'll find that they want to move sooner than they told you. We have kind of an adage in real estate, where we say, "Cut that time in half." If they tell you two years, it really means one. If they tell you one year, it really means six months.

People tend to push the timeline further on down the road, just like when you try to keep a clerk away from you in a store, and you say, "No, I'm just looking." Well, no, you're not just looking. You're buying very soon, or you wouldn't be in the store. Very few people just go to a store to browse. They ultimately want to buy, but they want to shop on their own for a while. And that's what these people, prospective seller leads, are saying. "We're not ready just yet. We don't want to feel obligated." This is a subtle way you can give them something without them feeling obligated. They can shop in the privacy of their own home, on their own time, and this should help them just look.

The seller lead auto-email drip scripts really should go to anyone who is thinking about moving in the near future. In fact, you could make the argument for someone who's not thinking about moving at all. People still like to be up-to-date on their neighborhood. That is why neighborhood home owners stop in Open Houses down the street. They still like to know what the other homes that come up for sale are like. They like to know their prices. They like to compare their home's condition and amenities to those homes. They like to see how fast things are selling. People are just generally nosy as well, and they like to look through photos of their neighbors' homes when they go up for sale. This is a way they can do that from the privacy of their den. So just about anyone that you know that owns a home could be set up on a seller lead auto-email drip script.

Again, it's a game of touches. The more people that we have on these drips, the more contacts we'll make, and that will just increase the likelihood that these people will use you to sell their next home.

Buyer Leads

Entering a buyer into the SOI Database is the most traditional use of the Auto Prospecting email drip tool and many agents are already familiar with it.

This is our script when someone wants to purchase a home, whether they are a first-time home buyer or repeat buyer. They have a rough idea of their price range, maybe even what parts of town they want to look at, or what neighborhoods or communities. They have thought about some of the amenities and features of the home they may have in mind, and number of bedrooms, size of garage and yard space.

All those things can be put in the auto search tool's search criteria by the agent. When that is done, we can always help people when they're just starting to look. That could be a year or two out. Again, we don't really want to discriminate too much based upon time frame because it costs nothing to put people on a search and start creating and adding value for them.

We can see when they're searching and how active they are. If we have a website with artificial intelligence, it notifies us when our buyers are actively looking on the website. Now even with the multiple listing service free tool, you can usually log in to see if they've saved searches.

You can look in and see that they have saved certain houses in their search box and are tracking them. When they log in, they can look at that house to see if it's still active, if it's sold, what price it sold for. You don't get notifications when they're actively looking like you would with a website CRM system that you purchase.

This script is more designed to help buyers search with your tool as opposed to the competing tools that are available to them when they just randomly go online looking for homes. And it's very important that you sell your tool to them, because often, people will just go online and search some of the many more public free websites out there, like Zillow. They need to be informed that those are limited websites where they don't get to see all the homes that are listed for sale, and not all the information contained in them is accurate.

What you are providing them is a direct feed into the multiple listing service, MLS, allowing them to see all the information that their real estate agent sees and in real time. When a new listing comes up for sale, they're going to be alerted and see that property at the same time the real estate agents see it. They will be up to date and everything will be active.

It's very important to inform them that homes they see on secondary sites are typically already sold by the time they get to the public free websites. Often the best homes, in the best condition, and at the lowest prices go too fast for those sites.

This is a great selling point for your site. It is a constant source of frustration to real estate agents that their clients call them and say they were on Zillow and they want to see this or that specific house. And the real estate agent says, "That house sold long ago. It sold two weeks ago." It's still showing up as an active listing that just hit Zillow and those other public sites. It really frustrates clients too, so we want to give them access. Use that opportunity to sign them in. The script and talking points we provide help clearly articulate that point – that they don't miss out on homes that have already sold quickly and we're going to give them free realtor access.

Once again, sellers have to buy somewhere else. Thus, for any prospect thinking about buying or selling, it should be your objective to get them on those tools on two searches. Develop prospective buyers and sellers at the same time.

So, we're keeping them up to date on the home that they have to sell, by putting them on a neighborhood search for their existing neighborhood. Then we're also setting them up on a search for homes that they may want to buy after their current home sells. That's just more contacts, more email, and more service and value you're providing to them, which increases the chances that they will want to work with you.

Closing to the Search Tool

4 Steps to Close

For years in real estate, a **three-step** closing was common. It was **contact, appointment, contract.**

We always tracked the **number of contacts** an agent makes, which means the number of conversations he has with people, whether it be SOI members, people in a farm or prospective buyers or sellers. And then we tracked them, to try to close them to an **appointment**, whether it is a buyer's consultation or sales/listing consultation. We would track the number of appointments to the number of **contracts,** which is usually a listing agreement or a buyer/agency agreement.

A **four-step** closing is now the norm. Rather than just going from **contact to appointment to contract**, we now have inserted a new step two, in between contact and appointment. We now go from **contact to search tool to appointment to contract.**

The internet has changed things for us, and added a new component called "home shopping". The internet has extended the representation process earlier in time, because now over 90% of home buyers start their searches online themselves. It used to be, they would **call a realtor** to go look at homes **as their starting point.** But now that they can search themselves, they start searching months earlier. Or they registered for a search on a website. Or they're already looking on their own somewhere else, on some other secondary website months and months earlier, because they can do it on their own now.

So now we want to try to capture that **contact** much sooner and get them in our **search tool** right away; we want to start working for them earlier in the process, to ensure that they ultimately do meet with us for an **appointment**. This gives us a higher chance of capturing their **contract.**

It just beats the competition to grab these online leads earlier in the home shopping process. "No, I'm just looking," is the mindset that a prospective buyer or seller has when they start to look online. They don't want to be obligated to a realtor yet. They just want to start searching for homes themselves, until they are ready to physically look at them, and/or meet with a realtor.

That's when they're comfortable being obligated. Just like when you're in a department store, and we start shopping around for different, let's say, belts. And you finally found the right color belt and the right size. It is then you need a clerk to help you buy it or find a different size or a different color; that's when you'll go to them. So, what we as realtors try to do, is help them find the "belt" in the "right size and color". We help them by reaching out to them and helping them just look for homes. So, we help them with their online search. We can refine that search. We can set them up on a better search. We can give them access to different homes or a smaller number of better-targeted homes.

Often, when people look online, they're looking at far too many homes. They might type in their city name and they don't want to miss any houses, so they sign up for a very high price range, a very wide margin, hundreds of thousands of dollars apart. They want all the homes in the whole city in a huge price range, and they start getting inundated with emails, and they can't look at them all, and they miss the actual homes that they might be interested in. So we can and must help them with that.

This search tool helps them look more efficiently. We're trying to get into a relationship and add value for them earlier by using the tool, and getting the right criteria in the tool for them is the first value we add. Now we have gone from contact to search. With every contact we make, we try to close them to a search. And as we've seen in the previous four sections, that could be anyone in your SOI, anyone in a geographic farm, anyone at all that's thinking about selling their home or about buying one in the near future. All are fair game, to close to a search. As we said before, it's a game of touches and the more prospects we have set up on searches, the more business we are going to get soon.

Think of it as trying to stretch the sales process out by going backward or earlier in time. Someone searching online might start in February and not approach a realtor until October. We're trying to, when we make contact and have conversation with them, "wash their windows". When you are in a major metropolitan area stopped at a red light, some random person will walk up to your window and start cleaning your window without your permission. they'll clean your window and you're there, whether you're telling them to stop or not, they're cleaning, and then after they're done, right before the light turns green and you can drive off, they look at you and put their hand out and expect payment. Now, often we don't pay them, but we do have an increased obligation. We feel a little bit of peer pressure and moral obligation to pay them, because they have already done work for us.

In a much more professional context, we're trying to wash their windows before they're ready to buy. And if we get them set up on a search tool, and they're constantly getting emails from us that are giving them homes that they're looking for or keeping them up to date on their neighborhood, they're going to feel a little bit guilty if they ultimately choose to buy or sell with a different agent, after we've been doing this for them (especially if we're doing a good job of following up with them, to ensure that they are getting the best use out of our tool). We'll talk about that in the next section.

For now, we need to understand the concept: Extending that service back in time, earlier in their transaction timeline, by doing educational, valuable, and free work for them. It's very similar on a much wider time frame, as if you actually sit down with someone before they're ready to sell and give them a price opinion, or offer them some vendors to do some work in the house to get it ready for sale before they've even agreed to let you sell it. Once you start doing work for them, there's an increased likelihood that they're going to use you to list their home for sale. "Pre-qualified and pre-approved" by a mortgage lender is a similar context that creates a mild sense of obligation; there's an increased likelihood they're going to use that lender.

Make Lead Follow Up Constructive

Lead follow up is going from contact to search to appointment. We're going to use the search tool to do lead follow up. When we make a **contact,** they're just a lead that we want to try to ultimately get into the **search** because that then takes us to the **appointment.**

We don't want to rely on just the emails. The emails are going to do a lot of the work automatically for us, assuming they're engaging with them, clicking on them, opening them, and going to look at the properties. A website CRM system tells us when they are looking at these properties, or we log into the MLS to see if they are using the search tool.

We are still going to follow up with them every now and then to 1) get their feedback on how they're liking the tool or 2) if they are receiving too many emails, ask them if we should refine and narrow their search to a more manageable amount of homes. Because now, they are starting to learn the different price ranges of the different neighborhoods. And they're saying, "Nah, we don't like those houses, let's focus on a higher price range," or, "We really like that side of town, let's see more of those properties."

Because now that they're getting emails, they're starting to be more alert, more aware. And their radar is up for different neighborhoods. Parents probably learned more about local school districts. We can start getting their feedback, following up, seeing if we want to further refine or modify their search.

We may find out that they're not getting enough emails, which means maybe their search criteria is too limited, we need to expand into a larger geographic area or increase the price range. We could increase the size, or bedroom/baths, expand the window of their search criteria to encompass more homes, etc.

So, we keep calling, and we keep following up, and looking for ways we can add more value and further "wash their windows" to build rapport and do what we call "nurture the lead" over time. We'll often call these follow up contacts "nurturers", because we're constantly coming from contribution.

We never want to push too hard, because they are still "just looking around, thanks". But we do want to probe enough to ensure that they are getting value; to make sure they are still in the market. And there are a number of ways we can do that. One of the most common is by trying to help them out with financing. No one really wants to sit down with a lender (painful). They'd much rather look for homes first (pleasant). They never really want to do that until they're ready. We don't say, "Hey, if you do find a home, let's get you pre-qualified so you'll ready to buy it." That's not usually an enticing conversation for someone who's still "just looking". So, we want to tie in the mortgage into how knowing their financing will help them focus better on the right type of homes.

In a nutshell, we'll usually try to explain, "Hey, would it help you, while you are looking for homes, if you knew what your monthly mortgage payments would be based upon each home that you see come up for sale?" If they hear that, now, suddenly, talking financing is an open topic. Often the purchase price means nothing to them, because they're not paying cash for their home. They really care about their down payment and their monthly payments.

We say, "If you meet with a lender, you can pick which loan program you like, and we can get a rough idea of what your down payment and monthly house payments would be, depending on the purchase price you see. A nd that might help you look at the best homes, with more information. It might help us refine our search criteria." You might suggest that you'll have a mortgage broker that you know and trust give them a call; let them talk even over the phone, to give them a rough idea of the budget they can afford.

All of a sudden, it sounds very easy, and you're trying to help. You're moving them forward, getting them closer to being ready to buy. You are getting them excited, too, about home buying. Or, if we're talking to a seller lead, they say, "Yeah, well, we have a lot of work to do around the home before we put it up for sale." That's when you might suggest that you could swing by and help them with some ideas, and maybe some cheap or quick ways to get it done. Or you could offer some of your preferred vendors who have worked with many of your past clients to help them get it done quickly, and be affordable for them.

You are coming from contribution. You are adding value.

You are their teacher, their go-to resource more and more.

You are making their search easier and more pleasant, more exciting.

In little ways like that, we're helping them and continue to wash the windows for them, to build more rapport and a trusting relationship, so that slowly we move them forward to an in-person **appointment**, and ultimately, a listing **contract**, or a buyer-agency agreement.

If they're not looking to buy or sell for a year or two, you might just call them every couple of months. However, if you know they're looking to buy or sell in a few months, you might start calling them every other week. So, do that lead follow up as a customer service, based upon the degree of urgency they have, before they're set to move.

The search tools give us something very, very easy to follow up with. Lead follow up, otherwise, without using a search tool, is rather challenging and time-consuming, because we're just going to be calling them, and virtually saying, "Are you ready yet? Are you ready yet?" That gets a little bit awkward, to say the least. The tool gives us something to call about. We can call about customer service, on how they're liking the tool. "You know, I've noticed that you've saved a few houses. I've noticed you've been on the website recently." If you have a website with CRM, you're getting notifications of when they're on the site. If you call them while they're on the site, you have an increased likelihood of them picking up the phone and talking to you about their home search.

So, it gives us a reason to call, something to service, which is their home search tool. We want to lead follow up. That's where they always say, "The money is in the lead follow up." And the search tool helps us do that. We still add value and come from contribution while moving them forward from **contact**, all the way over to **appointment** and **contract.**

Process for Setting Up and Contacting Each Day

Daily contacts are with your SOI, a geographic farm or any prospective leads (buyer or seller leads).

Let's start with your SOI. This process will hold true with any of these groups or categories of prospects. With your SOI, you have started by setting them up on searches and then shortly thereafter, calling them to let them know you did so. You'll notice all our scripts are geared that way. We're not asking for permission; it's very different to get permission to send someone an email. We want to let them know that we set them up on a search and then follow up.

Often what agents will do is we'll have them set up on 5 or 10 searches per day. And that can take a while, especially if it's your sphere of influence, your SOI because they all live in various locations. So we have to go into our website or the MLS and set up individual searches based upon each of their different home addresses. It may be faster with a geographic farm, but with an SOI, we must set up searches all over town depending on where they live.

We set up our predetermined number of them (that could mean five a day Monday through Friday, or 10 a day Monday through Friday). Then we'll quickly **call them all** to let them know and tell them that we'd love their feedback on it.

Let's say our goal is to do 10 a day. If we do 10 a day Monday through Friday, that's going to be 50 a week, and if there's four weeks in a month, that's gonna be **200 people in a month set up on these searches and contacted.** However, many people are in your sphere of influence database, your whole SOI will be set up on this system and contacted by phone every two months. They are all on a constant contact from either the MLS or your website going forward indefinitely. They'll constantly be getting exposed to you, your name, your logo. You'll repeatedly be contacting them.

We usually want to set them up and contact them each and every day until they're all set up. And again, we wanna be sure to be purposeful about that. Pick a predetermined number and ensure that we hit that number every single day.

Now, an automated voice mail service is an alternative for those of you out there who have too large of a database or are just adamantly opposed to making phone calls yourself ... It's not as effective as a phone call. **A phone call is the most effective contact that we make to members of our SOI or geographic farm,** because you'll get leads right then and there, and it's a great way using your voice live and in person, to build rapport and nurture someone. This said, you can import the phone numbers of your entire database into an online service that leaves automatic voice messages that bypass their phone, and a voice message appears in their voice message inbox. You pre-record that voice message with your own voice reading the script. So, instantly, everybody in your SOI will receive a voice message telling them to watch out for this new email that you set them up for.

Not everyone realizes that this is an automated service, but it is obvious to others. At least you're letting them all know and performing a touch. **It's just not nearly as impactful as having a live conversation with someone** as far as a database touch goes. But if you've got 1,000 or 1,500 people in your database, it may not be feasible to call them all, so an automated voice message would work. Or if you're farming a farm neighborhood of 500 or 1,000 homes, an automated voice message is another way to introduce this plan to them. Make your voice as professional and firm and confident as you can, and be sure to practice your script several times before making the final outgoing recording.

It's also a good idea to send out a mailer enumerating your six value proposition bullet points. You could send a mailed postcard to everyone in your SOI or in a farm neighborhood to let them know, "Hey, be on the lookout for our new search tool. Watch for my email on this." And another way to make a different, diversified channel of communication to contact them, the same postcard could really be set as a digital image and sent in a social media or Facebook private message to everybody that maybe lives in your farm or everyone that is in your sphere of influence that you happen to be friends with on Facebook.

We really want to set up and systematize this process so that everyday we're setting up the searches, we're contacting by phone, or if not feasible, broadcasting a direct voice message. We can also send out mailers with an online mailing service, or via social media.

NEIGHBORHOOD AUTO EMAIL DRIP SCRIPT:

Sphere of Influence (SOI) or Geographic Farms

"Hi, it's [AGENT NAME] with [REAL ESTATE COMPANY], I wanted to give you a heads up that I've set you up on our new Neighborhood Update Tool and would love to hear your feedback on it. My clients really love it. When one of your neighbors puts their home up for sale, you'll immediately get an email with all the listing information and photos of the home. This way, you'll be able to:

1. *Look through all the **photos of your neighbor's homes;***

2. *Compare the **amenities, features & size** of the listings to your own home;*

3. *Know the **price of each new listing** to get a rough idea of the current value of your own home;*

4. *See **how quickly each home sells**, and the **prices that they ultimately sell for;***

5. *This will give you a good idea of **how the value of your home is increasing** from month-to-month;*

6. *It will also **keep you up to date** on your local neighborhood's market conditions.*

"I really think you'll find this customer service tool useful since most of my clients already do. But if for some reason you decide that you'd rather not receive these updates, you can unsubscribe yourself or just simply reply to an email and we'll discontinue it for you. However, I'd love to hear what you think about it first.

"All that I need from you is to verify that I have the correct home address and email address for you. Sound good?"

GEOGRAPHIC FARMING AUTO EMAIL DRIP SCRIPT:

Phone & in-person contacts, email & mailer content

"Hi, it's [AGENT NAME] with [REAL ESTATE COMPANY], your [NEIGHBORHOOD NAME] expert.

"I wanted to give you a heads up that I've set you up on our new [NEIGHBORHOOD NAME] Neighborhood Update Tool and would love to hear your feedback on it. Many of the residents in the neighborhood are using it and really love it. When one of your neighbors puts their home up for sale, you'll immediately get an email with all the listing information and photos of the home. This way, you'll be able to:

1. *Look through all the* **photos of your neighbor's homes;**
2. *Compare the* **amenities, features & size** *of the listings to your own home;*
3. *Know the* **price of each new listing** *to get a rough idea of the current value of your own home;*
4. **See how quickly each home sells**, *and the* **prices that they ultimately sell for;**
5. *This will give you a good idea of* **how the value of your home is increasing** *from month-to-month;*
6. *It will also* **keep you up to date** *on the* [NEIGHBORHOOD NAME] *neighborhood's market conditions.*

"I really think you'll find this customer service tool useful since so many of your neighbors already do. But if for some reason you decide that you'd rather not receive these updates, you can unsubscribe yourself or just simply reply to an email and we'll discontinue it for you. However, I'd love to hear what you think about it first.

"All that I need from you is to verify that I have the correct home address and email address for you. Sound good?

SELLER LEAD AUTO EMAIL DRIP SCRIPT:

Prospective home sellers, move within 2 years

"Hi, it's [AGENT NAME] with [REAL ESTATE COMPANY], I wanted to give you a heads up that I've set you up on our new Neighborhood Update Tool and would love to hear your feedback on it. My clients really love it. This tool will really help you stay educated about your home's value and your neighborhood's conditions leading up to whenever you are ready to move. It might even help you decide when you want to put your home up for sale!

"Here's how it works: when one of your neighbors puts their home up for sale, you'll immediately get an email with all the listing information and photos of the home. This way, you'll be able to:

1. *Look through all the **photos of your neighbor's homes;***
2. *Compare the **amenities, features & size** of the listings to your own home;*
3. *Know the **price of each new listing** to get a rough idea of the current value of your own home;*
4. *See how **quickly each home sells**, and the **prices that they ultimately sell for;***
5. *This will give you a good idea of **how the value of your home is increasing** from month-to-month;*
6. *It will also **keep you up to date** on the [NEIGHBORHOOD NAME] neighborhood's market conditions.*

"I really think you'll find this customer service tool useful since most of my clients already do. But if for some reason you decide that you'd rather not receive these updates, you can unsubscribe yourself or just simply reply to an email and we'll discontinue it for you. However, I'd love to hear what you think about it first.

"All that I need from you is to verify that I have the correct home address and email address for you. Sound good?

BUYER AUTO-PROSPECTING SEARCH SCRIPT:

Prospective home buyers

*"The most desirable homes listed at the lowest prices sell the fastest, so you don't ever get to see them on Zillow and other secondary websites. **Homes on those websites are actually the homes that most people did not want.** You see all home listings are initially listed in the REALTOR®'s Multiple Listing Service (MLS) online database of homes for sale. Then the listing information is sent through digital feeds to other secondary sources, and then on to these other websites. This is why the information on these sites is often incorrect and a week or two old. So that's why websites like Zillow do not have the same number of listings as our MLS does. If you are looking for home on Zillow you're just seeing the leftovers that no one else waned. Are you following me?"*

*"Plus, many offices, companies, and associations of REALTORS® do not allow digital feeds to go to secondary websites like Zillow. **So not only do you miss out on the homes that have already sold quickly, but there are many active listings that you can't see at all.** Does all that make sense?"*

*"So, if you want to **see all the listings the minute they go up for sale and get FULL REALTOR® ACCESS,** I can easily set you up on our buyer search tool so that **you can see what the real estate agents see, as soon as they see it.** You can **look at the homes online in the privacy of your own home, on your own time, with absolutely no pressure or obligation.** I can even set the system up to send you email notifications the minute new homes hit the market that fits the specific criteria you are looking for in a home. If you happened to want to see the inside of one of them, you can just reply to the email or call me, and we'll get you inside quickly. Would that be a benefit to you?"*

*"This way you'll also be able to learn about the prices of homes in different neighborhoods to **become a more informed buyer.** You'll start to **see what's a good deal and what's not, how quickly certain homes sell in different areas and price ranges.** Once you see what you can get for your dollar, you'll also be able to drive around on the weekends and check out some of the neighborhoods on your own time. Look at the school districts, nearby shopping, and other amenities. You can take your time with this if you want. How does that sound?"*

ACTION STEPS:

1. **Set up** five members per day of your SOI on **neighborhood** automated email drip search campaigns, and do this **Monday through Friday.**

2. **Call** those same five people that you just set up on the neighborhood automated mail to let them know you did so. Use the neighborhood auto email drip script. Read the script and ask them for their feedback. **Take notes of what they say.**

Top producing real estate agents must continually find ways to both grow and contact their SOI Referral Databases. The trick is to find and keep only *effective* ways – and 'effective' means 'that which grows my SOI Database'.

Social media networks like Facebook now provide a very time- and cost-efficient means when appropriately used and when you focus on building your SOI Database. Social media can help rapidly increase the size of your SOI Database and allow you to systematically stay in contact with your SOI members. The trick, again, is using it effectively for your business-building, and not get caught up in spending hours per week just reading and 'recreationally' (rather than strategically) posting.

As you've surely noticed by now, making **40 contacts a year** to each member of your SOI database is challenging – yet not all that hard! In the early stages of setting up your SOI Contact Plan, it can seem both time-consuming and expensive, because you have not yet reaped the benefits of that work.

Keeping up with your annual SOI Contact Plan to earn **1 closed transaction for every 7 people in your SOI (7-to-1 ratio)** takes self-awareness of your resistance to following any sort of plan or pre-set activity schedule – until you remember the 90/10 aspect of the SOI Plan. Contacts are 90% automated and pre-scheduled; 10% of the Plan is you, on the phone, connecting with your SOI members.

Grow SOI through Social Media

BEWARE: Too many startup businesses in too many industries believe that using Social Media is the one and only way they need to grow their databases – and these naïve entrepreneurs could not be more wrong!

One way to grow your SOI (once you have scheduled the basic SOI Contact Plan tactics of emails, mailers, and phone calls), is to use social media according to a strategy. You do not begin with social media! You have already birthed your SOI and grown it as shown in earlier Modules.

Here we discuss Facebook, but the strategy is the same for other platforms. We give details for the strategy later in the module, but in a nutshell, this is your strategy:

Transfer your Facebook friends to your SOI Database, along with their known email addresses, telephone numbers and physical addresses. They become part of your SOI Contact Plan.

Often, real estate agents are connected with many people on Facebook who are not yet in their **customer relationship management (CRM)** systems. With this strategy, you will transfer their contact information into your SOI Database/CRM, and turn them into SOI members.

Since there is not a good way to export, sync or otherwise move these Facebook friends to your CRM with contact information for each friend, we have developed an easy method to systematically add Facebook friends to your CRM.

First watch this video on *Transferring Facebook Friends into a Client Database* to learn this step-by-step process. **Take notes as you watch:**

https://youtu.be/jCGtLqqrYdU

Personal Facebook Direct Message Script

Now it is time to transfer Facebook Friends to your SOI Referral Database. Use the following Facebook Direct Message Script to quickly grow the number of people in SOI.

"Hi, it's (YOUR FIRST NAME). How have you been? I'm updating my real estate database and I'd love to send you something over the holidays and from time to time. My real estate business was amazing last year, but I need to do a better job of staying in touch with people I know. So would you mind replying with your current home address, phone number and email address to help me out?"

The formula is a basic one:

Intro + Reason + Request for Help + Request as a Question

Be sure to end with a question, as it's a conversation for them to respond to. If there's no question, there may not be a response.

Engage with your SOI on Facebook

The best way for agents to generate real estate leads on Facebook doesn't cost money and doesn't involve frequent posting about real estate business, either. Instead, successful agents use this powerful social media tool as a means to interact and come from contribution with their Facebook friend's posts on a regular basis.

The process is simple: You listen and respond rather than talk and hope for a response. The more you stay in contact with the people you know, the more you are likely to generate business from your Facebook friends who become part of your SOI Referral Database.

Mega Agent Lisa Archer attributes a large part of her success in **selling over 600 units over the past 2 years** to a system she has developed to increase her engagement with people that she has grouped in different Facebook Friends Lists. Before we examine this simple system on how to generate leads on Facebook in detail below, watch Lisa explain the process herself in the following video. **Take notes as you watch:**

https://youtu.be/zg78zsos3l0 (video w/ Lisa Archer)

Lists Organize Your Messages

Facebook *lists* provide a great way for agents to come from contribution and be helpful. You can regroup any number of your friends into lists that you label as appropriate. Some of your lists, right on your Facebook page, will be "Referral Network Friends", "Seller Leads", "Buyer Leads", "Preferred Vendors Friends". This is a way to send a message that is appropriate to one category but not another – imagine that the message you send to a Seller Lead list is not the same one you'd send to Referral Network friends.

Social Proof Builds Business

Social Proof is a major reason people read their social media friends' postings. What is *'social proof'*? It is proof that a business's claims (great product, lowest price, money-back guarantees are honored, etc.) are true ... because your Facebook friends say they are. If a social media friend – and preferably many friends – have said good things about the product or service, their friends are more likely to buy ... and much more likely to avoid buying if the comments are negative.

You can use this phenomenon to your advantage. Offering assistance helps you be a connector for Facebook friends that seek 'socially proven' referrals for home improvement, local entertainment and dining, community information or anything related to their personal needs. This will also show the importance you place on customer service and helping others.

As a result, your online presence will provide a sharp contrast from agents that use Facebook just to repeatedly ask for business.

The graphic below illustrates one way agents can implement a daily agenda of social media work. It is a 10-10-5 exercise for your posting actions on social media.

Likes or emoji reactions

Comments on posts

Post shares or personal messages

Social Media Strategy

Defining your goals for using social media from the beginning to grow your SOI is critical to your success. Social media can help 'build your brand' – or, in other words, 'establish your reputation'. Don't let your usage of social media sabotage your reputation!

Here is some food for thought, especially for agents who have only used social media 'recreationally'.

1. Social media of all platforms is about creating relationships. It is all done through posts.

2. Predetermine the type of posts you add (your Post Strategy). Give value. Come from curiosity. Start many posts with "in my experience as a real estate agent, ..." when appropriate – but without asking for leads/referrals. Educate and inform when you can. The algorithms that are built into Facebook are rating your individual posts based on measurements like reach, interaction, and types of content. Post too much with no interaction and there's a chance the value of following posts could be lessened, and you'll show up less frequently in your friends' feed. Just as you gave serious thought to each of your email messages in your

SOI Contact Plan, give thought to the types of posts that bring value to others.

3. Ask if this is an activity a trained assistant can do. What are you looking for and what type of response/post do you give? Brainstorm together.

4. Decide how to mark Facebook (and other social media platforms) in your CRM, because unless you track the returns of these efforts, you cannot decide if it is a good source of new SOI members for you.

5. Above all, schedule this activity like an appointment. Don't get caught in the web of wasting time in surfing posts that are of no interest to your business and its growth.

Generate Leads with Friends Lists

Don't use social media only to generate buyer/seller leads. Grouping Facebook friends into lists with categories like Preferred Vendors, Friends in my CRM/SOI Database, Nationwide Referral Agents, etc., helps ensure that you can *appropriately* engage with your friends' posts on a daily basis. In other words, you won't send the same message to a referral agent in your network that says the same thing as a message to an SOI member already in your Database. Grouping in categories helps your message bring value to its reader.

Note that Facebook puts only the posts that you interact with the most at the top of your news feed. Typically, **real estate agents interact with the posts of different local agents and others who are equally _unlikely_ to give them business.** This is a waste of your time and energy. This puts the wrong people at the top of agents' Facebook news feeds and hides the people that will actually refer them business far down at the bottom.

Creating Facebook Friends Lists avoids this mistake. Spreading friends out in different lists helps you see everyone's posts so that you can *Like, Comment* or *Connect* with them offline to stay top of mind.

Steps to Create Lists in Facebook

Note: Facebook revamps its interface periodically, but the following was true at time of publication.

1. Simply open your home page on Facebook, and on the left toolbar, scroll until you see the heading "Friend Lists."

2. Once clicked, you'll be brought to a page with the "Friend Lists" title, and a display of all your current friend lists.

3. You'll be able to create your first list by clicking the button at the top labeled "Create List", which will open a new smaller window labeled "Create New List."

4. Label the list with an appropriate title that will identify them by any number of themes

5. Populate this list with your Facebook friends.

6. To search through all friends in a bulk fashion, click "Create" which returns you to your Master Friend Lists page, and click the title of your new list.

7. Once this page opens, in the upper right corner, click the button labelled "Manage Lists" and select "Edit List" and a pop-up will open, allowing you to see the current members.

8. In the top left of this new window, click the button that reads "On this list" and change it to "Friends" which will give you catalogue of all your Facebook friends.

9. Search through and click once on each person you believe will be a great destination for messages designed for the list.

10. Once finished, click "Finished"

11. From here on, any post you write on your page, you'll be able to choose the delivery audience, simply by clicking the button next to the "Post" button, which defaults to "Public."

12. Choose "Specific Friends", which will prompt you to type in the name of your specific list.

Library of How-To videos on Creating a Custom List on Facebook:

https://goo.gl/WUFDqP

When you create social media as an appointment in your agenda, note that you need to do regular reviews of how you're doing. Look at your CRM listings of new SOI members that Facebook has generated for you. Are the results respectable or non-existent? Without a plan for what you're doing, there's a likelihood that you'll spend more time and energy than you have available. Conversely, you don't want to dismiss social media out of hand, because the results could be far more interesting than you now imagine.

1. **Create an "SOI" list on Facebook.** Then scan through each of your current Facebook friends for whom you have complete contact information and **add each friend to your SOI Facebook Friends list.** That happens right in Facebook as described above. That means you have qualified that Facebook Friend as a member of your SOI Referral Database.

2. Add this individual to your CRM. You have decided that this person should be in your SOI Referral Database and receiving your emails, mailers and telephone calls from you.

3. Create other **Facebook Friends Lists** (Preferred Vendors, etc.). Scan your friends and add each one to the appropriate list.

4. **Identify missing contact information.** As you scan through all Facebook friends, identify the friends that qualify as SOI members, but for whom you do not have complete contact information. This is likely to be most of them! **Send each of them a personal message (PM) over Facebook using the script to ask for their contact information**. Tell them you would like to add them to /update them in your SOI list.

5. **Build Your Lists:** Repeat steps 1 and 2 once a week to keep growing your SOI Database from your Facebook Friends.

6. **Schedule your Social Media activities as appointments.** Time block 30 minutes in your calendar 3 times weekly. This may not seem like enough time at first, but the work you can do will be cumulative, so keep at it only for the allotted time. **This time is used only to add new members to your SOI Database and to post appropriately to those in each Facebook SOI list you have created.**

MODULE 9

The Buyer Lead Conversion Process

Your consistent focus on both growing and contacting people in your SOI Referral Database isn't only about building a book of business for the future. You've likely already learned that by making these contacts, you generate a significant amount of referral leads of individuals, families or even businesses looking to buy or sell real estate right now in the present. Thus far we have concentrated on making contacts to generate leads, so now we shift our focus to converting leads from **contact** to an in-person buyer consultation **appointment.**

Your Business is Defined by Your Behavior

Do you consider yourself a professional? Do professionals drop everything to hop in the car and show a property to a total stranger the minute their phone rings? Top producing agents understand the importance of conducting an *initial buyer consultation appointment.*

What is it? That caller is a 'lead' not a current client of yours; you don't know each other yet. He is a lead potentially interested in buying a property. The consultation appointment is an interview of sorts allowing you to properly set expectations and prepare clients for the home buying process at the outset of the agent-client relationship. It is when you start to build a relationship on a new level that arises out of the name-recognition relationship you began with (and that put this person in your SOI database in the first place).

These buyer consultations also serve other specific purposes. In order to maintain agent safety, screen prospective buyers, determine client needs, and create a foundation for the agency relationship, it is essential for real estate agents to take the time to conduct buyer consultations in the office prior to showing property.

Do Buyers Really Know What They Want?

What do buyers typically want from you when they make their first contact? Buyers initially want to either see a specific property or obtain information about it. Thus, they don't typically want to take the time to meet for an in-person buyer consultation. They want to get what they want from you and get off of the phone – just like customers entering a department store who will automatically tell the store's greeter, "Thanks, I'm just looking" after being asked if they can be helped.

Imagine a patient going to a doctor stating that he has already self-diagnosed himself and knows what medication he needs, and "Please write me that prescription, thanks, bye-bye." Many home buyers erroneously believe they don't need to tell an agent their 'symptoms' prior to looking at properties. They don't think about what happens if they see a well-priced home they want to buy. Are they pre-qualified? Is their existing home up for sale? They often put the cart before the horse and miss out on homes they want to buy because they aren't in a position to make an offer that has any hope of actually being accepted yet.

1. The Initial Conversation with a Buyer Lead

Confident professionals are not people pleasers, which is why it's crucial for agents to take control of these initial conversations with buyers to conduct a proper diagnosis with the confidence of an alert and well-trained doctor. A good doctor would not give a patient pain killers or antibiotics just because the patient wanted them. Instead, he would first ask a series of probing questions to inform himself and determine the patient's needs. Only then would he prescribe a remedy in the patient's best interests.

Top agents do this too, through active listening. This is simply asking a question, then validating that you have heard buyer responses correctly by repeating them back to the buyer. It sounds like this, "I understand that you are now seeking a 4-bedroom home in the ___ area as near the public school of ___ as possible. Is that right?" Agents should carry on by asking follow-up questions to expand the amount of specific information, validating each new statement with a similar question, and further ascertaining more of the buyer's situation and needs.

Agents use a Buyer Lead Sheet to guide the series of questions and to centralize all the prospect's responses. Review the Sample Dialogue provided below to see how the agent validates each request and then proceeds with a question in each exchange.

Sell Your Product to Get the Appointment

Once your control of the conversation has been established, you should then attempt to explain that the buyer's current method of looking for homes is not the most effective. Buyers typically look for homes on secondary websites (Zillow, etc.), by visiting open houses, looking at advertisements, or just by driving around and calling numbers on yard signs. It is important to educate buyers that a Multiple Listing Service (MLS) auto-prospecting search will enable them to see all homes listed on the market by all agents the minute they come up for sale.

Agents should use this auto-prospecting service as the reason to 'sell' a meeting <u>in person</u> for the initial buyer consultation *appointment*. Thus, marketing this feature to potential clients is an equally important part of the conversion process. Once the appointment is set and the Buyer Lead Sheet is completed, then it's time to have buyers speak with your lender prior to meeting with you at the buyer consultation.

The following is a breakdown of the scripts, dialogues and talking points to help you take buyers through this 4-part process from initial contact all the way to setting the in-person buyer consultation appointment.

1.1 - Take Control and Come from Curiosity

Sample Dialogue:

> BUYER: "Could you tell me the price of the home located at 123 Main Street?"
>
> AGENT: "Yes, 123 Main Street, that' a great house. Are you're looking to buy sometime soon?"
>
> BUYER: "Yes we're thinking of moving to this side of town and that house looks really nice. How much is it?"
>
> AGENT: "It's beautiful home for sure. Tell me, are you renting right now? Or do you own a home?"
>
> BUYER: "We're renting until we can find a home to buy near my parent's house."
>
> AGENT: "Yes being close to family is important for sure. How soon are you looking to move?"

Notice how you gently and politely take back control of the dialogue and ask the questions to collect the information you need. You do this before answering the prospect's main question of 'the price of 123 Main Street'.

Use the Buyer Lead Sheet to help guide you and keep the questions coming. Once we get into questions on the Buyer Lead Sheet about what they are looking for in a home, move on to number 2 below:

1.2 - Give to Get with MLS Auto-Prospecting

"The most desirable homes listed at the lowest prices sell the fastest, so you won't ever get to see them on Zillow and other secondary websites. Homes on those types of sites are actually the homes that most people did <u>not</u> want. You see, all home listings are initially listed in the REALTOR®'s Multiple Listing Service (MLS) online database of homes for sale. Then the listing information is sent through digital feeds to other secondary sources, and then on to these other websites. This is why the information on these sites is often incorrect and a week or more old. So that's why websites like Zillow do not have the same amount of listings as our MLS does. If you are looking for a home on Zillow, you're just seeing the leftovers that no one else wanted. Are you following me?"

"Plus, many offices, companies, and associations of REALTORS® do not allow digital feeds to go to secondary websites like Zillow. So not only do you miss out on the homes that have already sold quickly, but there are many active listings that you can't see at all. Does all that make sense?"

"So if you want to see all the listings the minute they go up for sale and get FULL REALTOR® ACCESS, I can easily set you up on our online platform so that you can see what the real estate agents see, as soon as they see it. You can look at the homes online in the privacy of your own home, on your own time, with absolutely no pressure or obligation. I can even set the system up to send you email notifications the minute new homes hit the market that fit the specific criteria you are looking for in a home. If you happened to want to see the inside of one of them, you can just reply to the email or call me and we'll get you inside quickly. Would that be a benefit to you?"

"This way you'll also be able to learn about the prices of homes in different neighborhoods to become a more informed buyer. You'll start to see what's a good deal and what's not, how quickly certain homes sell in different areas and price ranges. Once you see what you can get for your dollar, you'll also be able to drive around on the weekends and check out some of the neighborhoods on your own time. Look at the school districts, nearby shopping, and other amenities. You can take your time with this if you want. How does that sound?"

"Great, all that I need to do is briefly meet with you in person to set you up on our system and then you can leisurely browse for homes on your own time. Would 4:00pm today or 2:00pm tomorrow work for you?"

1.3 - Complete the Buyer Lead Sheet

SCRIPT:

"Thank you! I just need to ask you a few more quick questions before we meet. This will help me get you set up on our online platform ahead of time, so you can be in, out, and on your way faster when we meet in person. Is that OK?" "Great! Thank you."

Proceed with remaining questions on the *Buyer Lead Sheet* to determine if they have a home to sell first. If they do, switch to *Seller Lead Sheet* and proceed accordingly. Otherwise, find out if they have been prequalified with a lender. If not, proceed to section 1.4 below.

1.4 - Now Set the Lender Appointment

SCRIPT:

"When you search for homes online, would it be of benefit to know what your down payment and monthly payments would be based upon each home's asking price that you see?"

"To most people, it's more important to know what their monthly payments would be when initially selecting home search criteria, not to mention later on while they are comparing homes that they are actively searching for online. Does that make sense to you?"

"Depending on the type of loan program you select, these down payment and monthly payment amounts can vary significantly. I can have my lender give you a call before we meet to help you get a rough idea of what each of these amounts will be based upon in the loan programs you might select. There will be absolutely no cost or obligation on your part, it will just help you get more clarity about the homes you actually want to see in your online search. How does that sound?"

"Not to mention, if you do see a home that's priced well, it will likely sell quickly. So you'll have your financial ducks in a row with a lender pre-qualification letter to provide to the sellers. That would increase the likelihood of your offer being accepted. Make sense?"

"Great! Here's my lender's name and number, and I will provide your contact information to her as well. This way you can both start trying to get in touch with one another prior to our meeting so that we will be able to further refine your online home search based upon what you learn from her. Sound good?"

"Wonderful. I'm looking forward to meeting you in person!"

Now contact the lender to ensure that they speak with the buyer prior to your buyer consultation appointment. Ensure that the lender knows to proactively contact you if they are unable to reach the buyer so that you can help follow up.

2. Conduct the Buyer Consultation

When conducting the in-person buyer consultation, it is preferable to hold it in your real estate office for the sake of convenience, safety and professionalism. However, if this is not feasible, it can also be conducted at a title company, mortgage company, coffee shop or even at the buyer's residence. It is also helpful to have a computer with you, so that you can set the client up on an MLS auto-prospecting home search *while you are meeting with them.* It may also be a good idea to have your lender present if the buyer has not yet been pre-approved.

The subject matter of the buyer consultation appointment should cover the 6 following areas.

2.1 - Market Conditions

At a minimum, real estate professionals have a duty to use due diligence in the representation of their clients. Thus, making prospective buyers aware of what they can expect as a buyer in today's market is essential.

Talking points should **cover local market conditions:** the available inventory, buyer negotiating power, interest rates and local list price to sales price ratios. If proper expectations are set up front, buyers have an increased likelihood of getting the home they want without climbing a steep learning curve or missing out on several desirable homes.

2.2 - Loan Pre-Approval

Since many home buyers are eager to start viewing homes before determining their borrowing power, agents must educate their clients about the impact that being pre-qualified for a home loan has on purchase negotiations. Buyers that know what **down payment amount and monthly payment** they can actually afford will also be able to make much more informed decisions about the homes they consider. Consequently, pre-qualified buyers are confident and more inclined to make offers in an expedient fashion. In the event that your buyer has been unable to meet with your lender, use this opportunity to set the meeting before showing them property.

2.3 - Define the Agency Relationship

Understanding **agency relationships** is not only beneficial to clients, but also very helpful in preserving commissions down the road. Real estate agents should prepare buyers for specific situations that might jeopardize the relationship and commissions in the future. For example, home buyers need to be instructed on how to handle encounters with For Sale By Owner (FSBO) homes, open houses, and new construction builders. Buyers should be made aware of how the agency relationship is impacted in these situations, and what consequences it may have on representation and commissions.

2.4 - Ask for Referrals

The highest rate of referrals always comes from ongoing relationships with clients who are **actively in the process of moving.** Similar to how people shopping for cars notice every other vehicle on the road, clients preparing to move have a heightened awareness of other people looking to do the same. Consequently, this topic often dictates many of their social and professional conversations, which puts your chances of receiving referrals at an all-time high during the home buying process.

SCRIPT:

"By the way, most of my business comes by word-of-mouth from past clients. It's how I prefer to run my business. So, if you know anyone looking to buy or sell a home this year, would you mind referring them to me? Can you think of anyone now?"

2.5 - Establish Home Criteria & Search Process

The determination of the location, price range and features that a buyer is looking for in a home often serves as the central focus of a buyer consultation. However, it is equally important to establish parameters for the process in order to **avoid an endless search** that renders ineffective and confusing results. Further, time management is often the most pressing issue that agents representing buyers face in their practice. Since buyers' agents are often forced to work nights and weekends to accommodate client work schedules, effective scripts that set boundaries for showings are vital for the preservation of a balanced life. Since some clients simply enjoy looking at a lot of houses, they often lose sight of the goal of actually purchasing a home. In order to avoid this dilemma, it is important to keep clients in a **'buying mindset'** throughout the home search – before setting them up on MLS auto-prospecting.

2.6 – Sign the Exclusive Buyer Agency Agreement

The key to obtaining a **signature on a buyer agency agreement** is to present it in a matter-of-fact manner as if it must be signed prior to moving forward with showing homes. An exclusive buyer agency agreement entitles the agent to a commission when the client purchases a home within a specified time period. So if an agent expects to be compensated for the time, expense and expertise associated with locating and showing properties, the buyer agency agreement should be presented at the initial buyer consultation presentation **as if it were the agent's policy that the agreement be signed by all clients.** Use any of the following scripts and objection handlers to ensure that you always get exclusive buyer agency agreements signed before showing property.

SCRIPTS FOR PRESENTING THE EXCLUSIVE BUYER AGENCY AGREEMENT

Script 1 – "It is our policy to have you consent to me representing you as your agent before we start looking at homes. By signing this you are just agreeing to that."

Script 2 – "I'm required to have an agreement between us to be able to act as your agent and show you homes. I just need your signature to get started."

Script 3 – "By signing this agreement you are authorizing me to represent you and look out for your best interests throughout the home buying process."

Script 4 – "In order for me to help you without possible conflicts of interest, protect your confidentiality, and operate in your best interests, I am required to have you sign this agreement to represent you as an agent."

Script 5 – "My broker requires that I have my buyers sign this agreement, so I can get to work for you and be on your side."

HANDLING OBJECTIONS TO SIGNING THE BUYER AGENCY AGREEMENT

Script 1 – "Often times I find that if a buyer is uncertain about signing this agreement, it usually means I haven't answered all of your questions or there is something you haven't told me. Was there something you wanted to cover today that I forgot to ask you?"

Script 2 – "What is it that concerns you? Would it help if I stepped out of the room for a bit so that you two can chat privately?"

Script 3 – "Signing this agreement is actually our policy since I can't be 100% committed to you unless you are 100% committed to me representing your best interests."

Script 4 – "I sense a little apprehension. I tell you what, if we get to a point in the process where you don't like working with me, then I won't have a problem ending our agreement. I just ask that you let me know as soon as possible. How does that sound?"

Script 5 – "I tell you what, how about we look at a few homes to make sure you're comfortable working with me, then we can worry about signing it?"

BUYER QUESTIONNAIRE & LEAD SHEET

Buyer Questionnaire & Lead Sheet

Date: _____ Lead Source: _____

Name: _____ Spouse Name: _____

Property Address: _____ City: _____ State: _____ Zip: _____

Phone #s – Mobile: _____ Spouse Mobile: _____ Home: _____ Work: _____

Email: _____ Spouse Email: _____

Family / Children (include ages): _____

1. Have any other agents shown you homes? ☐ Yes ☐ No
   If Yes, do you have a signed agency agreement? ☐ Yes ☐ No
2. Is anyone buying the home with you? _____
3. Are you renting, or do you own a home? ☐ Homeowner ☐ Renter
   a) HOMEOWNER:
   - Do you need to sell your home before you buy? ☐ Yes ☐ No
   - Have you signed a listing agreement to sell your home? ☐ Yes ☐ No **If "No" use Seller Lead Sheet.**
   b) RENTER:
   - When does your lease end? _____
4. What date do you want to be moved by? _____
5. Are there any negatives to not moving by then? (suggest lifestyle sacrifices, job, costs, schools, family, etc.)
   _____
6. Tell me all the benefits of buying a new home: (dig deep & find out WHY?)
   _____
7. On a scale of 1 to 10, how would you rank your motivation to move? With 10 meaning you
   must buy as quickly as possible, and 1 meaning you're not sure you'll really buy anything: _____
   - What's missing? What would it take to make you a 10? _____
8. Do you know where you want to move to? _____
9. Will you be paying cash or getting a mortgage? ☐ Cash ☐ Mortgage
10. Have you been pre-approved by a lender? ☐ Yes ☐ No
11. How much will your down payment be? _____
12. What price range are you looking in? _____
13. How many BR: _____ Baths: _____ SqFt: _____ Stories: _____ Other: _____
14. What else are you looking for in a home? _____
15. Will anyone else be involved in your home buying decision? _____
16. "Thank you! I'd love to help you find your perfect home. All that we need to do is to set an appointment so that I
    can help you find the home you're looking for. Does 4:30 tomorrow or 5:00 Wednesday work for you?"

Appointment Date/Time: _____

DISC Behavioral Profile: _____ Why? _____

1. Contact all of your current buyer leads to attempt to **set a buyer consultation appointment** with each of them. Be sure to come from an attitude of 'giving to get', by using **MLS auto-prospecting** as your reason to meet in person.

2. Continue adding **5 new people to your SOI referral database per week** by adding them to your CRM or using the SOI Member Contact Form.

3. Make 5 telephone contacts per day to SOI members by using any of the scripts provided in our previous training modules.

Contacting people in your SOI Referral Database doesn't just generate buyer leads. You have an equal chance of being referred listings to sell property as well.

In the prior module, we explained how to convert the initial buyer **contact** to a buyer consultation **appointment**. Then we covered converting the appointment into a signed buyer's agency agreement, or **contract.** This very same process is applicable to seller leads as well. The key to moving seller leads from initial contact to a listing appointment, and then on to a signed listing contract is to tackle these steps one at a time in the correct sequence. We'll start at the beginning, by discussing how to convert seller contacts into listing appointments, then we'll move on to converting listing appointments into signed listing agreements.

The successful **conversion of listing leads to listing agreements** thus involves three distinct steps you always follow, and in this order:

1. **Contact** – initial telephone call
2. **Appointment** – in-person meeting at the seller's home
3. **Contract** – signing the listing agreement, often at the end of the appointment

Step 1: Converting Seller Leads into Listing Appointments

Don't get ahead of yourself. One of the major differences in skill between top producing listing agents and the rest of the agent population is the ability to convert seller leads into listing appointments. Far too many agents get ahead of themselves by trying to close the contract over the phone **rather than closing the appointment.**

For example, during the initial telephone call, sellers will often raise objections to listing such as:

- "We still need to do a lot of work to our home before we're ready to sell."
- "We need to find a home to buy before we're going to sell."
- "We don't really need to sell now."
- "We're planning on moving later on in the year, we're not quite ready yet."
- "We need to wait to be able to get a little bit more equity out of our home."
- "We can't afford to pay a full commission. How much will you charge us?"

These are not objections to meeting for an appointment at all!

All of the seller objections listed above are actually **objections to listing the property for sale now.** In other words, they are objections to signing a listing **contract**. Agents that get stuck in telephone conversations by these types of objections are getting ahead of themselves by trying to close the contract instead of the appointment.

Right Back at You

Instead, top listing agents use these objections as a reason to set the appointment. Focus on the appointment only in each response to an objection like these. You turn the seller objections back against the sellers by using them as a reason to meet to discuss the issues the sellers are having. Here are some ways the top producers do it:

- A seller that needs to find a home before they list should meet with you so that you can set them up on a Multiple Listings Service (MLS) auto-prospecting home search to get 'full REALTOR® access' of all the homes that are listed by all agents that meet their specific criteria as soon as they hit the market.

- Homeowners that still need to 'fix up a lot of things' in their home before selling could use your advice on what things to fix and what to leave as-is. Present your expertise as you explain which improvements bring a higher sale price and which ones do not. You can also suggest cheaper methods and products to make improvements, or even refer some of your preferred vendors to perform some of them.

- Sellers that need to get more out of their home or are otherwise waiting to sell might benefit from a Comparative Market Analysis (CMA) to be able to see what their home would sell or be appraised for in this market. You could also show them comparison listings that are active and pending to give them a rough idea of what their home will be worth later in the year as well.

- Concerns about commission are better explained and shown in person than discussed over the phone. Saying, "It's easier to show you than tell you" is a good way to lead into setting the appointment. Thus, you also present in person all potential costs associated with the sale in order to determine the amount of net proceeds sellers will have at closing.

Agents will too frequently lose listings to competing agents because they are unable to set appointments when they first speak with a lead. They assume that the seller isn't ready and don't want to be pushy by pressuring them to list now. So they wait with the hope that they will later be able to close the seller from **contact directly to contract, skipping the appointment step** in between. These very same agents are severely upset when they later learn that home was listed by another agent who was able to set the appointment and help the sellers much earlier in the process.

The key is to remember that you can in fact help sellers more by meeting with them in person – and sooner rather than later. Then all you have to do is communicate this point to them. Tell them, "It would be my pleasure to come to your home and answer all your questions. Seeing the property will definitely allow you to get more accurate answers, too." Sight-unseen answers would be guesses; eyes-on guesses are more on target.

Benefits of Using a Seller Lead Sheet

The first benefit to you of letting the Seller Lead Sheet guide the conversation is that you are in control of the conversation and how it unfolds. Control the conversation by coming from curiosity which is, in fact, based on your Lead Sheet questions.

The second benefit is visually showing your expertise and professional approach. Asking a series of questions pertaining to seller needs and circumstances by utilizing a **Seller Lead Sheet** shows your own preparation and expertise (you know the questions to ask), confidence, organization (you are using a pre-printed form) and professionalism (they see you write down their responses). It also demonstrates that you care about their needs. Therefore, it is important that you end every sentence with a question mark and avoid statements that end with periods. Moving down through the questions contained on a Seller Lead Sheet keeps the conversation focused and purposeful.

A third benefit of the Seller Lead sheet is that it helps to unearth possible objections that you will likely need to overcome during the in-person listing consultation later. Asking the questions on a Lead Sheet will prompt seller responses that reveal their objections (or their state of readiness to sell), such as:

- "Have you spoken with any other agents yet?" (Your competitors)

- "Have you thought about selling the home yourself?" (Commission objections)

- "Do you have an idea what price you want to sell it for?" (Price objections)

- "What price did you pay for your home and when? Have you made any improvements to it?" (Price objections)

- "How much do you owe on the property?" (Price objections)

- "When do you want to move?" (Lack of seller urgency objections)

- "What do you think you still need to do to the home before putting it on the market?" (Condition objections)

- "Why do you want to move? What happens if you don't?" (Lack of seller motivation)

Get in the Door

Often sellers just need to be reassured that by meeting with you they won't be obligated to list their home now or even with you. Remember, **the key during the contact stage is just to get the appointment**, so don't start worrying about getting the listing contract yet. Your odds of getting the listing will go up significantly the minute you meet with them face-to-face. In the meantime, it's important to try to disarm them about the purpose of your meeting. Here's how that might look:

Seller: "We're just not ready to even think about it until the kids are out of school in a few months."

Agent: "I can understand that. It's much easier to move when you don't have to work around a school schedule. Let me ask you, if I were to be able to show you how much your home is currently worth, and how much it will likely sell for over the summer, would it be of any benefit to you?"

Seller: "I suppose so, but I think it's better if we just wait till the kids are out of school."

Agent: "Sure. In the meantime, what if I set you up on our system to give you 'full REALTOR® access' of all the homes that are listed by all agents that meet their specific criteria as soon as they hit the market. This way you could look – in real time as they go on the market – at homes, without any pressure or obligation. You could do this in your free time, in the privacy of your own home. And whenever you are ready to sell, you will already have a good idea of what you might be able to purchase. Would that help?"

Seller: "That would be great, yes!"

Agent: "Excellent, when would be a good time for me to swing by? Would 4:00pm tomorrow or 3:00pm Wednesday work better?"

Seller: "Wednesday is better for me."

Agent: "Great! Just so that I can do a bit more homework and save us a little time on Wednesday, would you mind if I asked you just a few more questions?" (If they agree, you proceed with Seller Lead Sheet questions; if they'd rather not, just say you'll chat during your meeting. This again reduces the pressure or sense of obligation.)

Step 2: Converting Appointments into Signed Listing Agreements

Successful listing consultations start long before agents show up on a doorstep to meet the sellers in person. Top agents understand the importance of setting the proper tone with homeowners in advance of meeting. Providing sellers with a Pre-Listing Packet before the actual consultation helps subtly change the intended purpose of the meeting from information gathering to listing the home for sale. This way, **the conversion starts happening before you even show up.**

What is a *'pre-listing packet'*? It is a pre-printed, professionally assembled collection of introductory information for your leads. It contains background about you and some of your successful listings (sales), testimonials from past clients, a Preferred Vendor list, a Sell-Your-Home checklist, a bit of homework for the prospect and more.

The Benefits of a Pre-Listing Packet

Pre-listing packets take little time to prepare since the majority of the packet is pre-produced and standardized as your normal listing consultation anyway. Using a pre-listing packet sets, right up front, a professional tone and provides expectations about how you work and how the relationship will be conducted going forward. Those are time-saving advantages to you, but there are other benefits:

1. First, a pre-listing packet helps you stand out as more thorough and professional in competitive listing situations.

2. Second, it shows that you've already done some work for them – at no cost to them and at no obligation. This makes it harder for them to cancel your appointment or choose another agent in the meantime.

3. Third, effective pre-listing packets provide clients with documents or 'seller homework' to complete in advance and at their leisure, which saves time for everyone later.

4. Fourth, they also help sellers learn about you and local market information in their own time, which cuts down on questions later in the actual consultation.

5. Even if they haven't done the 'homework', or read the provided agent or market information, you can point to it during the appointment as you also respond verbally. This further demonstrates your degree of preparation (and how you have strived to save them time and provide value).

Packets allow clients to feel that they have done their own due diligence ahead of time, and thus, they can feel more comfortable signing the listing agreement on the spot during your consultation appointment.

Delivery of the Pre-Listing Packet

Delivery of the pre-listing packet can be done both digitally by email and in printed form for personal delivery, and indeed you should **use both formats for each potential client.** Packets must be provided on time and as promised to build trust early and further set the tone for the relationship. Personal delivery of a printed packet can be performed by the agent or an agent's representative (assistant, etc.); when an assistant shows up with a printed packet, this subliminally demonstrates that you are 'a real business with employees'. In the case of personal delivery, be sure to inform sellers in advance when it will be delivered. Use the following scripts for personal delivery of the pre-listing packet:

SCRIPT FOR SPEAKING TO SELLERS AT THE DOOR:

"Hello Mr. Smith, I'm Kathy with Annie Agent of ABC Realty. She wanted me to provide you with this information about your upcoming appointment with her. You're going to love working with Annie!"

TELEPHONE SCRIPT AFTER LEAVING PACKET ON DOORSTEP IF NO ONE ANSWERS:

"Hello Mr. Smith, I'm Kathy with Annie Agent of ABC Realty. I wanted to let you know that I left a packet on your front doorstep today with information about your upcoming appointment with Annie. You're going to love working with her!"

Pre-Listing Packet Contents

1. **Agent Biography** – Should be the first page behind the cover of your pre-listing package. Start building the relationship here by showing your experience, community involvement and your unique value proposition to demonstrate what sets you apart from other real estate agents. It's also a good idea to describe your local community involvement and some personal information about your family and interests. This helps them get to know you and feel somewhat connected to them before ever meeting in person.

2. **Examples of Homes You've Sold** – Put your best foot forward here by using homes that you've sold in the price range and location that you want to be known for. This is also an opportunity to show off your marketing materials by presenting the homes on templates for various property flyers, online ads, print advertisements, etc.

3. **Testimonials from Past Clients** – They illustrate the high level of customer service you provide and your ability to sell homes quickly at close to listing price.

4. **Marketing Plan** – Explain what you do to get homes sold fast and for the highest price possible. Whether you hire a professional home stager and photographer, make outbound phone calls to prospect for buyers, or hold strategic open houses, lay out the highlights of your marketing plan so that they know you are a pro-active agent working to get their home sold.

5. **Strategic Partners/Vendor List** – Include the names and contact information of the vendors that can assist clients with the sale of their home. Ensure sellers that you can hold these companies accountable to the highest level of customer service and fair prices since you recommend their services frequently.

6. **Checklist for Preparing a Home for Sale** – Give them this list of ideas and tasks to get them into action before putting the home on the market.

7. **Explanation of the Home Selling Process** – Provide a detailed timeline of the steps it takes to move from listing to contract and then contract to closing.

8. **Local Market Data** – Provide updated market data to give them a general idea about prices, inventory levels, days on market (DOM), and sales in their local city or community. These are general statistics not specific to their neighborhood. This is not intended to show them the value of their home as a comparative market analysis (CMA) would. A CMA should only be provided at the in-person listing consultation.

9. **Local City & Community Information** – Show that you know how to market your local area. Most of this information can be found on your local Chamber of Commerce website

or on entertainment and travel sites. Showcase here the community's best attractions: sports teams, landmarks, award-winning businesses such as restaurants, shopping districts, schools, entertainment, arts, etc. Use attractive photos, narrative and statistics. This content can also make your pre-listing package suitable for use with relocation companies and organizations looking for an agent to help them with recruiting prospective employees like hospitals and large national companies.

10. **Listing Consultation Homework** – Often included as a separate letter or attachment so that it stands out, this is a list of things for sellers to have ready prior to your actual listing consultation meeting with them. The list should include filling out any mandatory sellers disclosure forms, providing a key to their home and gathering copies of HOA documents, mortgage statements, title paperwork, etc. If you arrive at the listing consultation and you see these items on the counter, you can feel confident that your presentation is quite likely to move quickly towards getting the home up for sale.

Arriving at the Listing Consultation Appointment

Once you enter the home, it's important to set the tone for where you want to conduct your actual listing consultation before you actually tour the home to take a look at it. We recommend the kitchen or dining room table, seated relatively close together so that everyone will be engaged in the discussion. Sitting at a table creates a more formalized environment where decisions will be made and business will be conducted. **Don't conduct consultations on couches or chairs in a living room.** This is far too relaxed a setting with everyone further away from each other, feeling too relaxed to make meaningful decisions and commitments.

Touring the Home

There are two different schools of thought as to whether agents
should tour the home with or without homeowners prior to sitting
down at a table for the actual listing consultation. Since there
is good rationale for each approach, we leave the decision as
to whether or not to include sellers on home tours up to each
individual agent. Here are some of the benefits of each method:

Touring without Sellers: Proponents of touring homes without a
seller present appreciate the fact that touring alone allows them
to control the time and agenda. It also prevents sellers from
building up the attributes and value of their homes in their own
minds right before they start a discussion about listing price. It
can be difficult to get a seller to be realistic about their home's
value when they just spent thirty minutes selling you on all of its
features. Plus, touring alone gives agents the freedom to focus
on negative features that might need some work or adjustment
without offending the owners.

> AGENTS ADOPTING THIS APPROACH CAN USE THE FOLLOWING SCRIPTS WITH SELLERS TO HELP EXPLAIN WHY THEY PREFER TO VIEW HOMES BY THEMSELVES:
>
> - "Would you mind quickly filling out this quick Home Seller Information Questionnaire while I look through the home on my own; that way, I can see it through the eyes of a buyer, evaluate how updated it is and to see if there are any repairs needed that would prevent us from selling?"
> - "It helps me to view the home freshly like a prospective buyer would for the first time."
> - "This allows me to see certain things automatically like a buyer. Things like cobwebs, carpet fading or chips in the wall that you may no longer notice."

Touring with Sellers: The majority of agents prefer to tour homes with sellers present because it provides a higher level of comfort (you, the stranger in their home, are not just wandering around), and more time to build rapport and the relationship before sitting down at the kitchen table to talk about the more sensitive issues like listing price or commission. Plus, taking this time with the owners enables agents to learn about possible seller objections they might face in the actual consultation. They might learn that the sellers want to wait to list until the flowers in the back yard are in bloom, or that they attribute far too much value to the granite countertops they installed a year prior. Agents can then mentally prepare to overcome these specific objections in advance.

Sitting Down at the Table

After you have viewed the interior and exterior of the property and sat down at a table, you sit together. **It's crucial to avoid a long, drawn out tell-and-sell type of presentation** where you endlessly list all of your attributes and marketing efforts. For them to truly hear and believe these positives about you, **they must be engaged.** To be engaged they must participate, and to participate you must involve them by coming from curiosity and asking questions.

Converse with the sellers through a question-answer approach that engages them actively.

Once again, it is important to **avoid statements that end with a period and instead only ask questions that end with upward question marks.** After all, you have already provided them with your pre-listing packet so they should already have a good idea about what you bring to the relationship. Plus, asking questions about their needs shows your confidence in your abilities to market and sell the home while caring about their concerns.

Try starting out the conversation with one of the following questions:

- "Besides price, is there anything else you would like to know?"
- "Now I've got a lot that I can show you today, but before we get started, tell me what questions you have for me?"
- "First tell me, what concerns you most about selling your home?"

Asking questions about their concerns and needs regarding the sale of their home will start to uncover all of their objections to selling. Typically, these objections will be about one of the following:

1. Price
2. Timing
3. Condition
4. Commission
5. Motivation/Urgency to sell

Get them focused by getting these concerns out of the way first.

Starting out with questions helps uncover and isolate seller objections for you to overcome right from the start. Otherwise, it's very difficult for them to listen to you with their own concerns floating around in their heads, so it's ideal to bring objections to the surface early and eliminate/address them as soon as possible. In fact, agents who are diligent in using the Seller Lead Sheet in their initial telephone conversations with sellers will be likely to have a more complete idea in advance about the objections they need to uncover.

Conduct a Needs Analysis

Similar to how a doctor diagnoses a patient by asking a series of questions to learn about the patient's symptoms, real estate agents should take the time to learn about the needs and concerns of their clients throughout a listing consultation. For REALTORS® this process is called a **Needs Analysis.** In a needs analysis, agents guide the sellers through a series of questions. This demonstrates a higher level of customer service as you are uncovering the needs of clients while also tapping into the motivators that get them into immediate action.

Needs Analysis 1: The High Road

The first step in conducting a needs analysis requires agents to learn **what benefits their clients will get out of moving into a new home.** Whether they are moving for more living space, to be closer to family or to get into a better school district, agents must come from curiosity by asking a series of questions to completely unlock the 'why' behind the move. Understand that walking them down the high road is not about what the agent has to offer in a value proposition. Instead, a true needs analysis begins with a thorough line of questioning to uncover all client motivators.

In order to fully unlock client motivation, it is imperative to tap into the **emotions** they will experience after they have moved. How will being closer to their family make them feel? How will that change their quality of life? **People can't say 'No' to their own goals**, so it is essential to ask the extra questions to bring the emotion behind their goals to the forefront prior to making important decisions regarding the sale or purchase of a home.

Needs Analysis 2: The Low Road

What happens if your clients end up unable to move because they are unwilling to make necessary repairs or price their home correctly? Many agents will learn why a client wants to move, but few will walk clients down the low road to **help them self-discover the pain and dissatisfaction that will result from a failure to take**

specific actions. Understand that people move away from pain much more quickly than they move towards their motivators, so bringing the displeasure that will result from their inaction to the surface is often what gets them moving forward.

Needs Analysis 3: Weigh Action against Inaction

Ask them to make the decision here. **What is more important to them – the benefits they will encounter from moving or the discontent they will experience from inaction?** Remember, if they author it they will own it, so it is imperative that they self-discover their decision through questions. A way to ask this question might look like this:

"Remember that I work for you, so all I can do is provide you with information and let you make the important decisions. So what is more important to you, trying to test the market and gamble on a price that's $10,000 above market value or pricing it correctly to get the home sold and move closer to the rest of your family?"

This helps them frame the issue and makes their decision very clear. They are able to self-discover their own denial and quickly make the choice that is in alignment with their goals.

Needs Analysis 4: Handle Objections

Experienced agents know that objections are typically either fear (usually from lack of information) or excuses to avoid the uncomfortable actions that stand in the way of reaching their goals. So your key to success is to isolate the objections and weigh them one-by-one against the pleasure they will receive from moving. So, if clients express that they "don't want to give the home away" (sell at too low a price), simply ask them, "What is more important to you – being closer to your family or not having to give the home away?"

Repeat this 'either-or' type of question with each objection to show how each basis for inaction is not in alignment with their reasons for moving at all.

Sooner or later, there will be nothing left for you to do but obtain a signature on the listing agreement.

ACTION STEPS:

1. Contact all of your current seller leads who are waiting to sell – **attempt to set an appointment with each of them now.** Be sure to 'give to get' by offering to give them an opinion on the value of their home and/or setting them up on MLS auto-prospecting as your reasons to meet in person. Tell them you'll have a packet of interesting facts and information for them at the meeting you set up.

2. Continue to add **5 new people to your SOI referral database per week** by adding them to your CRM or using the SOI Member Contact Form.

3. Make **5 telephone contacts per day to SOI members** by using any of the scripts provided in our previous training modules.

SELLER LEAD SHEET

Seller Questionnaire & Lead Form

Date: _____

Name: _____ Spouse Name: _____

Property Address: _____ City: _____ State: _____ Zip: _____

Phone #s – Mobile: _____ Spouse Mobile: _____ Home: _____ Work: _____

Email: _____ Spouse Email: _____

Family / Children (include ages): _____

1. Have you spoken with any other agents? ☐ Yes ☐ No _____
2. Have you considered selling the home yourself? ☐ Yes ☐ No _____
3. Why do you want to move? _____
4. Do you know where you want to move to? _____
5. What date do you want to be moved by? _____
6. Are there any negatives to not moving by then? (suggest lifestyle sacrifices, job, costs, schools, family, etc.)
   _____
7. Tell me all the negatives of not moving at all? (same suggestions above)
   _____
8. Tell me all the benefits of buying a new home: (dig deep & find out WHY?)
   _____
9. On a scale of 1 to 10, how would you rank your motivation to move? With 10 being highly motivated: _____
10. When did you buy your home? _____ What price did you pay? _____
11. Do you know how much you still owe on it? _____
12. Have you made any major improvements to the home since? ☐ Yes ☐ No
    _____
13. Do you happen to have an idea as to what you think it's worth, or should sell for? _____
14. Do you have a price you won't sell your home below? _____
15. Tell me about the positive & negative features of your home:
    _____
16. How many BR: _____ Baths: _____ SqFt: _____ Stories: _____ Other: _____
17. How did you hear about me/us? _____
18. Are you interviewing any other agents? ☐ Yes ☐ No   Who? _____ When? _____
19. "Thank you! The next step is for me to take a quick look at your home and I can answer any other questions you
    may have. Then you can decide what we do next. How does that sound?" (pause)
    "Great! Does 4:30 tomorrow or 5:00 Wednesday work for you?"

Appointment Date/Time: _____

DISC Behavioral Profile: _____ Why? _____

MODULE 11 — Everyone Loves a Party

As a real estate agent, every activity you perform is to serve and develop your Sphere of Influence. Your goal is to earn their trust, have their mind-share, have them refer business to you, and bring you their own listing.

Each approach in your Contact Plan is devised to bring value to the SOI member – more knowledge, information about his home or neighborhood or the greater real estate market, and so on. It all serves to give you mind-share, but also to help prepare your SOI membership for an eventual home sale or purchase of their own … with you.

In the last module, we gave you insights on how to measure what is important (your Key Performance Indicators or KPI) and ways of not only tracking but reviewing and analyzing your results for improvement.

You might now just add a KPI called Events. Contact, beyond the Basic Contact Plan, takes on many forms, including events.

Without a system, without a schedule, without experience, it can seem overwhelming to keep adding to your Basic SOI Contact Plan. Additional time spent, greater amounts of cash spent, and the effort to do all of them can *seem* to outweigh the benefits. But in this module, we are going to show you how to easily add Events to your SOI Contact Plan – and encourage you to schedule some type of event each quarter, every year.

Each event constitutes an additional touch your make to your SOI database, and a diversification of your Contact Plan. Its additional competitive advantage is relaxed face time that you have with SOI members and that they have with you. They get to know you. Because of that trust, the guests you invite from your SOI database will be comfortable bringing guests to your event (which you encourage) and who will represent 'new faces' to you that grow your SOI database.

An event is a great way to build trust – if you remember that your professional behavior, even at a 'fun' or predominantly 'social' event, is being observed, and you act accordingly. Part of your professional persona is throwing a *well-organized* event.

Events to Create a New Touch with Your SOI

Those from your SOI database who have been clients are invited to a Client Appreciation event. You can reserve some events for your Referral Network – those industry professionals who comprise your Preferred Vendor List, which is given to your SOI members to help them keep their properties in good repair or upgraded by proven and trusted experts.

Such events can take the form of quarterly parties, summer picnics, happy hours, fund raisers for which you are sponsor, etc.

The success agents are seeing by employing **events** in their Contact Plans is notable. Orchestrating an event involves becoming a Party Producer, more than a Party Planner. You have a checklist for the event; every time you again hold such an event, you just pull out your checklist of action items. Part of the checklist is a clear indication of not only who to invite but how you do its promotion.

Hosting events to your SOI members is part social, and part science. You bring together people with a shared interest, thus even a large group of people can connect with each other. You announce a start and end time to the event, a measured amount of time together, which thus communicates respect for others' time. You hold the event in a neutral, comfortable environment, such as a hotel party room. It is an invitation-only event to show consideration for your privileged relationship with each guest.

You simply create a repeatable blueprint for each type of event, and over the years, use the blueprint – with its checklists and so on – to recreate your successful events with little lost time.

The 5 W's: Choose Your Event Concept

Every plan starts with a concept. An event for whom? What type of event? When can we best hold it? Where? Why hold it for those guests or at that venue? The Who, What, When, Where and Why define your concept.

Who? Will you invite only buyers/sellers whose transactions closed in the past 12 months? Will it be an event only for your Referral Network?

What? Are you organizing a breakfast event or an after-work drinks event? Is it a fund-raiser in support of a widely-supported cause?

When? What month and day of the week seem most appropriate? Friday evenings are generally to be avoided, as are Monday evenings – but maybe those turn out to be the best choice for your own event.

Where? The place you hold your event depends on the above three answers. 'Who' tells you how many guests you plan on; the 'What' determines what amenities you need at the venue; the 'When' is all about venue availability. Possible event venues include public outdoor parks, professional sports events (tailgate parties or box suites), restaurants, wine bars, or even in a new luxury listing in conjunction with a promotional open house.

Why? The feel of these events is that the environment is intimate and comfortable. It is decidedly not a seminar or 'pitch' opportunity. It is a chance for you to mingle, connect in a comfortable setting, and build a relationship outside the office.

Then comes the **How Much** issue. How much can you/should you budget? You see this is in relation to your **What and Who.** You will have a different budget for each type of event, size of its guest list, and its related expectations. Depending on the event, some of your Referral Network might kick in a contribution in kind or in cash or personnel to man the event. Always ask if you believe it is appropriate – not just to have a smaller tab yourself. Just one or two commissions generated as a result of holding the party typically justifies the expenditure as 100% your own

Finally, you determine **Staff** needed to create the event. Can you use your current staff? If not (because you do not yet employ staff), research how to find 'temp' workers or even family and friends to man your event. More than one event has seen Boy Scouts as waiters!

Promoting SOI Appreciation Events

A great client appreciation event is one extra way you add to your SOI Contact Plan in which mind-share is solidified and referrals are earned.

Events are beneficial both to you and to your guests in the following ways:

- The value events bring to your business is largely in the communication you deliver to organize the event – how you extend invitations, your attitude in talking up the event, etc.

- Organizations hosting parties are viewed somehow as businesses of more seriousness, are seen as prospering, because you are willing to commit to projects of this scale.

- No matter how many guests show up, it's a sign of appreciation, but the power is in the giving. Your attitude is joy and appreciation for all those who did arrive – they will never know how many declined or did not come, so treat those who do very well!

- You have an opportunity to introduce your clients to each other for their mutual benefit – one SOI member may be a singing teacher and another seeking lessons for one of his children. It can be as easy as that.

- You're in control of the promotion, the communication, about the event and your enthusiasm is key. Your attitude that 'you love these events' is key. Your perspective that it is for 'appreciation' rather than a blatant attempt to drum up more business is vital.

There are numerous ways to promote client appreciation events. A blend of all of them might be needed, while in other cases, one approach is enough.

E-mails

1. Save the date email
2. Event invitation email
3. Event reminder email
4. Post-event "Thank you for coming" email for all attendees
5. Post-event "Sorry with missed you last time" to those not in attendance, with your invitation to the next event

Telephone Calls

1. Event invitation call
2. Event reminder call
3. Post-event "Thank You" call
4. Post-event "Thank you for coming" call for all attendees
5. Post-event "Sorry with missed you last time" call to those not in attendance, with your invitation to the next event

Group Texts

1. Reminder texts with directions and details – to all who have RSVPed they are attending
2. "Thank-you for coming" texts with a promise to let them know about your next event

Mailings

1. Event invitation mailer
2. Post-event "Thank you" notes
3. Post-event invitations to next event

Facebook & Social Media

1. Timeline Posts
2. Create an Event Page, Group Page or Friend's List
3. Personal Messages
4. Don't forget Pinterest, Instagram, & YouTube if your SOI uses them

Social media scheduling tools like Buffer, Hubspot, or Hootsuite will ensure that your messages go out on their scheduled days, and ease the organizational burden. This allows you or your assistant to prepare/draft posts well in advance. These pre-scheduled posts might include 'save-the-date' messages for your next event – and sent to the appropriate social media SOI list you created in a prior module.

You or your assistant should also track 'non-response' from your guest list. Schedule making phone calls to re-extend the invitation, since you really don't know the open rate of any of your email/ text/mailer invitations.

NOTE: Don't forget your biggest cheerleaders on every one of your guest lists! Be sure to include invitations to your entire staff (even the part-timers), your closest friends and family, and any and all of your business/real estate Mentors, Advisors or professionals involved in your success such as your CPA or attorney.

NOTE: Don't forget how you have been building your SOI Database! It is through people who know people who know people – who all know you or come to know you by name. Encourage each invited SOI member to bring 'a likeminded guest' – that is, someone sharing an interest in real estate for his/her own property, seeking a new home, thinking about selling a current home. Capture their contact information at the time of the RSVP without fail when your SOI contact tells you who he is bringing and call immediately to thank the guest for coming (and to complete the contact information, as well as add the individual to your SOI database and Contact Plan right away). Make a point of meeting your SOI member's guest at the event and chatting.

Features of Your Event

You've decided upon the Who, What, When, Where and Why and sent invitations. Now your checklist invites you to decide what *features* you create for this event. A 'feature' is something special that happens at the event. A breakfast event *naturally* includes breakfast foods and coffee, teas, etc., so those are not features. However, a breakfast event that involves being photographed by the town newspaper photographer and potentially interviewed by a local reporter is a 'feature' of that event!

Some other potential features:

- **Raffles and contests** for prizes (often donated by vendors). Raffles are a great way to get contact information from those attending your event: make it a drawing where residents get tickets by providing their name, email, physical address, and phone number. With a ticket, they'll have a chance to win a prize that's been announced. The more valuable or "cool" the prize, the more your guests will want to participate in your raffle – and buy one or more tickets each.

- **Photos/Videos.** It is important to shoot as many photos and videos at the event to later post on social media – and include in post-event emails and other promotional materials. People love to see great pictures of themselves and to say, "I was specially invited" to your event. Include this in your posting: "Our special guests included ..." Be sure you assign someone qualified with a camera to shoot photos and videos at the event.

- **Something for the Kids.** If you look through your database and find that a number of your contacts have a family, consider making at least one of your events each year a kids-welcome and kids-friendly one. Offer face-painting, organized events (races, games), bouncy houses, etc. This might be a good way to receive more Yes RSVPs.

Hosting the Event

As the host, you and your staff or helpers are encouraged to interact with guests and manage all aspects of the event for your guests' enjoyment – and this benefits your 'brand' and thus your business through reputation development.

Assign someone to

- Watch for arrivals and welcome them and their guests.
- Note who has left.
- Check on refreshments and replenish them as needed.
- Purpose: If collecting books, canned goods, donations - keep a tally of who gave what for your Thank-you notes.
- Networking: Assign all your helpers to keep notes of new things they learn about your SOI members so that you can follow up in a timely way. Note all referrals given, introductions made to any of you, etc.

Keep flyers on hand as well as invitations for your next scheduled event – this helps to keep momentum high, and to front-load your guest list for the next event.

The Post Event Review

With the last of the guests gone, and the clean-up complete, an important portion of the work still remains – your post-event review and schedule of calls. Items that may show up on your checklist could be:

- Review of the attendance roster, who attended or didn't
- Handwritten thank-you notes, with invitations to the next event
- Photo review, tagging, and social media posting
- Post-event calls to those who RSVP'd yet didn't show
- Data entry of new guests into your database from the event list you made

- Raffle awards, and data entry from registrants, with e-mail "thank-you" and highlight of next raffle
- Charity drive/Raffle/Contest results, as appropriate to the event
- Referral tally and follow-up scheduling
- Thank-you notes to staff, vendors and all helpers (yes, even family!)
- Review of promotion methods that worked, didn't work, and an adjustment for next time

For more insight, check out this resource:

 Video: https://youtu.be/Q2VVjGCu0_w

MikeGunselman

This film explains how to generate business by conducting and promoting multiple client and vendor appreciation events a year.

1. **Plan an SOI Client Event:** Set up the Who, What, When, Where and Why.

2. **Develop Your Promotion Plan:** Map out and schedule your varied streams of communication and book them on your calendar. These will be part marketing, part prospecting, so consider time, cash, and energy involved.

3. **Find your Helpers:** Contact vendors, staff members, friends and family for help, as needed. Support also takes the form of event checklists, and drafting the messages you wish to send at each stage of promotion.

4. **Plan Your Review:** Review not only for the SOI database growth you may have reaped, but for the 'feel' of the event, your (and your helpers') sense of how it felt, was received, and how smoothly it all went. Make a list of corrections you want to make for a smoother event next time.

MODULE 12 Do You Have the Time?

By now you're probably realizing that keeping your marketing department open every day is more difficult than it first seemed. Making daily contacts to your SOI referral database generates leads, those leads need to be converted, and an ever-increasing number of transactions need to be serviced. Now you might understand why we stress that ONLY those agents who are able to SUCCESSFULLY complete 40 contacts a year according to their database contact plans will obtain the 7-to-1 conversion ratio from their SOI. It's simple, but not as easy as it appears.

It Won't Come Naturally

Just because you have learned that your SOI referral database of 250 people should generate 35 transactions per year (250 ÷ 7 = 35.7) doesn't mean you'll stay motivated to hold up your end of the bargain. Motivation wanes over time – regardless of the reward. If money was an adequate motivator, there would be wildly successful people everywhere. Desired monetary results simply won't put enough fuel in the fire all by themselves. Most everyone wants a better body or health, but very few will commit to uncomfortable activities they don't naturally like to perform to improve their well-being.

How resistant are you to this SOI Contact Plan??

The more quickly you become *self-aware* of your real degree of *resistance* to dedicating daily time and determination to the SOI Plan, the more quickly you'll make the necessary changes to your natural behavior in order to be successful. The good news is that **you do not need to like the activities, you just need to want the results.** If you want the results badly enough, you can modify your natural behavior for limited periods of time by putting controls in place that lead you to act purposefully day-after-day.

If you are having difficulty (resistant to) making telephone contacts to members of your SOI each day, it's essential to put measures in place that increase the likelihood that you will do so going forward. Of course, this will involve some change, and deviation from your habitual behavior can be uncomfortable. The key is to prevent yourself from quitting before you even get started. Here is a sort of mantra to help you stay motivated:

"90% of my SOI Contact Plan is automated. This is only my daily 10%...It is only my daily 10%."

Any trick or tool to help you stay the course is a good one to use daily! Let's look at more ways.

Reserve Your Judgment

Since most agents don't enjoy contacting their database, they subconsciously make time for everything else until they don't feel like there's time to keep their marketing departments open. **It's not because they don't have time, it's because they don't want to do it – this is more resistance manifesting itself.**

If time were truly an issue, then how do multitudes of top producing agents find the time when they are closing transactions on a weekly, or even daily basis? They have the same 24/7/365 that you do.

They have the same database CRM that you do in many cases. Are they just that much faster or more efficient? **No!** But they do prioritize and make good decisions with their time. They do have ways of counteracting their resistance when it pops up and tries to sabotage them. Successful agents have experienced the results from conducting lead generation activities consistently. They remember those successes when resistance kicks in. This motivates them to perform tasks that they ordinarily would dislike.

Plus, who are you to say that you don't like contacting your SOI? Do you even know what it feels like to successfully contact an SOI Referral Database of 300 people 40 times in a year and close 43 transactions (300 ÷ 7 = 42.8) in a year? If you do, then we apologize. But if you have not done it yet, then pay close attention. **Be careful not to judge whether or not you enjoy doing something until you are proficient at it.** Until you make enough contacts to hone your skills, increase your efficiency, and ultimately get consistent results you don't realize how easy contacting the people you know can be.

Many people aren't too crazy about ice skating – especially if they do it only once per winter. Until they take a real lesson, do some focused practice and become skilled at skating, they resist it! And why wouldn't they when the first trip to the ice skating rink involves an endless hour of falling on hard cold ice. Yet after a single lesson followed by several practice sessions, skaters can't wait to get back on the ice to experience the sheer joy, freedom and beauty of the sport. The difference in enjoyment between novice and mastery level skaters is enormous. Yet if experienced and skilled ice skaters had made a knee-jerk judgment about whether they liked the sport or not on their first day at the rink, they would've never learned how amazing it can be.

Put yourself in that skater's shoes as you learn the lessons presented in this book, practice them with focus, and become skilled at the different steps of a top-producing SOI Contact Plan.

Put Customer Service in Its Place

As we have explained, successful businesses have marketing departments and customer service departments both operating simultaneously. It's essential to prevent the time it takes to perform business servicing activities from eroding the time allotted for income producing activities conducted by your marketing department. Otherwise your number of clients will soon level off or decline and you'll have no clients left to service anyway. Even though **performing daily business generation activities is the one duty that can be directly correlated to agents reaching their desired production and income levels,** they still typically allocate far too much time instead for customer service.

Income Producing Versus Business Servicing

For incoming-producing success week after week and year after year, **the 80/20 rule** should prevail every day:

Spend 80% of your time doing what produces income; spend 20% of your time (or less!) servicing the business the 80% efforts created.

This said, in real estate we prefer to go with the more factual 90/10 version of this rule. Most real estate agents spend 100% of their time on business servicing activities that only get them 10% of their desired results. Instead, agents should focus more time on income producing activities that will account for 90% of their goals. Hire assistants to perform the 10% that is rote, administrative and non-incoming producing.

For example, if an Annie Agent regularly sells **15** homes annually but now wants to increase that number to **40** homes a year, she will have to sell an additional 25 homes next year. If Annie had only focused on providing amazing customer service to the 15 clients she represented last year she might have gotten 1 or 2 additional transactions through word-of-mouth referrals from those 15 clients. This increase in production would amount to less than 10% of 25 additional homes she needed to sell to hit her goal. Which is why only **10% of production goals can be attributed to business servicing activities.**

Conversely, let's assume Annie Agent had focused more time working on a **Database Contact Plan** instead. She could've then expected to receive a 7-to-1 conversion ratio from her 160-member SOI Referral Database and thus would have sold 23 more homes (160 ÷ 7 = 23). That alone would've gotten her to 90% of her goal of 25 additional homes sold!

Income producing activities account for 90% of an agent's goals.

Don't Throw Yourself Under the Bus

If you know that spending time on income producing activities gets you 90% of your desired results and business servicing will account for only 10%, why on earth do agents always prefer to default to the customer service activities? It's once again because humans are people pleasers by nature and no one is looking out for you and your goals. Even though reaching your preset objectives may improve the lives of your family and loved ones, no one is telling them that you aren't performing the tasks you need to complete in order to increase your income. They all see how busy you are, but not what is keeping you so busy. If they knew that you were really spending 100% of your work time on customer service and not on 'selling', they'd want to know why you are wasting your time!

Agents do this all the time. They rush to pick up a phone call from a seller while they are supposed to be making their SOI contacts. Disclosures and other file work is completed throughout the day by the agent rather than by an assistant – until no time or energy is left to reach out to SOI members. Agents schedule buyer walkthrough inspections during time allocated for lead generation activities. The list of bad time usage decisions can go on endlessly.

Agents do this because no one is watching them, but **their clients are always watching.** No one is ensuring that agents do the things necessary to hit their goals. Yet a client will know how quickly an agent calls them back. Buyers will see if agents jump to show them a property on the spot. As a result, agents typically throw themselves right under the bus to meet client needs. Unfortunately, their goals get run over with them, and their family and loved ones feel it through smaller income and belt-tightening at home.

We're Not Asking for Much

Don't worry, it will all fit in your day.

Understand that **time fills the space allowed**, so if you have only business servicing duties to perform it _will_ take you all day to do them. But if you start your day with 2 efficient hours of income producing activities you will generally perform all of your servicing tasks much more quickly to still get home at the same time.

That's all we ask. **Just 2 hours of focused business generation time per weekday** at a minimum. So, if you consider a 40-hour work week as your standard, we're just suggesting that you **protect 10 total hours per week for business generation**, and you'll still have 30 hours per week to service your existing transactions. So 75% of your job will still be devoted to providing a high level of service to your clients.

If you are an 80/20 purist, here is a feasible version for you of the 80/20 rule: spend 4 times more time creating new business than servicing current business. And learn to call upon your assistant to do non-income-producing tasks.

Let's Break Down the Numbers

If 2 hours per day doesn't sound like much to build a business, look at it these two ways. First, your SOI Contact Plan is 90% automated – that is work you no longer have to plan into each of your days. Second, there are 52 weeks in a year – 50 working weeks with your vacation time. If you multiply 5 week days in a week (Mondays – Fridays) by 50 weeks you will get 250 weekdays in a year. If you keep your marketing department running for 2 hours a weekday (making those phone calls), just multiply 2 hours by 250 weekdays to give you **500 total hours of lead generation activity in a year.**

Add the **automated** marketing and contacting you are achieving with your Plan to the 2 hours/day of **active** marketing you commit to – can you imagine the results this can produce for you?

Automated Marketing + Active Marketing = A Large Number of Closed Transactions

Let's break it down even further by using Annie Agent. Assuming her SOI Referral Database of 160 people was being contacted by email and mail in an automated manner through her customer relationship management (CRM) system. That leaves her just telephone calls to make on her own. If her Database Contact Plan requires her to call each person in her database 3 times per year, that means she needs to make 480 total calls (160 people x 3 calls each = 480 total calls) in a year. As mentioned previously, she has 250 weekdays to make these calls. Therefore, she will only have to make **2 calls per day** (480 calls ÷ 250 weekdays = 1.92 calls per day) to stay on track with her goals.

Why do you resist making those 2 phone calls each day?

At first, Annie Agent resisted this task. So, she added a line item to her assistant's job description: **"Verify the names of the calls Annie has made and don't let her leave the office any given morning – or do anything else – until at least the minimum number of calls is made."** She created an 'accountability partner' for herself, in the person of her salaried assistant. That is determination! But it was also an effective plan that worked to short-circuit Annie's natural procrastination.

As you're aware, agents don't need 2 hours per day to make 2 telephone calls. However, many agents have larger databases. Other agents perform additional forms of business generation activities to prospect for new business, in addition to marketing to their SOI Referral Database. The following graphic illustrates how the daily schedule of a top producing REALTOR® might look:

The Magic Morning

Top producing agents who consistently market to their databases almost always do so in the morning, just like Annie Agent. So if success truly leaves clues, that's when you should be conducting your income producing activities too.

Perform your lead generation calls first thing each work day.

As you can see in the REALTORS® Daily Schedule graphic above, **lead generation is the first thing to be performed each day**. Notice that emails aren't checked (Annie Agent's assistant did that), phones aren't answered and paperwork is not complete (indeed, this is the assistant's job, too) until the marketing department 'closes down' at 11:00am. If followed, as it was by Annie Agent (many thanks in the beginning to her assistant) this sample schedule leaves no room for interruption.

This is also why the graphic above leaves an hour blocked from 11:00am to noon for business servicing right after lead generation time ends. Many times agents will jump to answer their phone during lead generation time because they are worried they won't have time to get back to the caller later. Let your assistant or your message service take the calls. By preserving this hour for business servicing, agents know they don't have to interrupt their income producing activities. They know they will have time to get back to any caller within an hour or two – and most people are happy you call them back that quickly:

Every call in real estate can be returned within a couple hours without offending anyone.

Understand that there must be no distractions while your marketing department is open. Answering a single phone call can take your business generation completely off its rails for the day. It just takes your answering one call to cause the need to make another, then another, then you'll need to draft a few emails, and so on. You know the drill. You probably also know how frustrated it makes the rest of the day for you. However, if you have kept your marketing department running without interruption, almost no crisis you encounter later in the day can get you down. The feeling of accomplishment you will experience carries with you until it's time to go home.

You're No Longer Free in the Mornings

One of many reasons why agents make their contacts first thing in the morning is **there are fewer distractions in the morning.** Buyers typically don't want to see property first thing in the morning and sellers usually want to conduct listing appointments in the late afternoon or early evening.

Agents also have more energy in the morning to make contacts with enthusiasm and that promotes better engagement. Whether you consider yourself a morning person or not, it's scientifically proven that the neurons in the brain function with a higher intensity after a full night's sleep. This is why we also hear that you should tackle your most difficult tasks first thing each day. Your mind and body simply have more energy early in the morning, which increases the likelihood of opening up your marketing department consistently each day.

So start adopting a new mindset that you are no longer available in the mornings. When inspectors want to schedule their inspections, when buyers want to view property, when scheduling closings, when an appraiser wants to be let into a home, simply respond with:

> "I have an appointment at that time, so how about 3:00pm that afternoon?"

As long as you maintain a good calendar, this will be a true statement. It's no one else's business who that appointment is with or what it's for either – or if you even have one. This time is for your marketing department to operate, so protect this time with all of your efforts. As we'll cover shortly, using a calendar properly will further help fortify your business generation time.

Lead Conversion Time

In the REALTOR® Daily Schedule graphic above, you see that an hour is blocked off from 1:00pm to 2:00pm for Lead Conversion. Too frequently agents will talk with people thinking about buying or selling a home soon, but fail to follow up frequently enough to convert them into an appointment, and ultimately a contract. By preserving a set time in your day for this, agents are ensured to keep in contact with active leads and continue to attempt to close them to appointments.

As we explained the processes for converting buyer and seller leads into appointments in Modules 7 and 8 respectively, the key is to come from contribution and try to find a way to help leads by meeting in person with you. However, seller and buyers aren't always ready to meet when you call, so we adopt the process of **nurturing leads** by staying in touch and attempting to help them until they are willing to meet and get started. The key is to be consistent when nurturing leads. We typically recommend reaching out once a week to try and add some value to them and build rapport.

A Well-Kept Calendar Drives Business

Put simply, a thorough calendar is another major difference between top performing agents and the rest. Most people use a calendar only to show appointments with other people. As people pleasers, we would certainly never want to let others down! Then we keep a To-Do List of items that we want to accomplish for ourselves. It's almost as if we prioritize everything that's important to us (customer service) in our calendar, and then the things we will get to when we have 'spare' time (business generation) are off to the side, on a secondary list.

From now on – and knowing that spending time on income producing activities gets you 90% of your desired results and customer service will account for only 10% – the practice of keeping a separate To-Do List must stop.

Successful agents understand that protecting their marketing departments is even more critical than business servicing appointments. They see it as crucial to merge everything on their To-Do Lists into a single "Have-To-Do List" otherwise known as their calendars. **This is a commitment since all tasks are assigned AT THE HOUR they must be completed.** This makes them much more efficient with their days. It causes them to work purposefully with a higher level of energy.

No one naturally moves through the day with high efficiency in getting their tasks completed with urgency. As previously stated, using a calendar to detail everything you do starts out as a purposeful activity that is very uncomfortable at first. However, once the skill is perfected and the habit is set, agents love the results. They love feeling productive, accomplished and successful at their profession.

Time Blocking

'Time blocking' is simply making an appointment with yourself.

Putting your To-Do List items and lead generation times in your calendar is setting actual appointments with yourself that must be time-blocked and protected from business servicing needs. So honor thy calendar and try not to stand yourself up!

Also be sure to set clear start and end times in your calendar as well. Hold yourself accountable to starting and stopping on time too. If you give yourself the leeway to start making your contacts 15 minutes late to take care of some other matter, you will set a habit that will solely permit you to start later and later. It's crucial that you hold yourself accountable to the activities that drive 90% of your goals.

Remember that business generation is your priority during your work hours, but making time for your family, spirituality, and health should be your priorities in life. Time blocking in a calendar helps protect your time and gives you a more balanced life in general. So **start by blocking out all of your personal commitments in your calendar** for a few months out. **Then add in all of your business generation time blocks each weekday morning** and fit them around your personal commitments when needed. Now when business servicing needs come up you can fit those appointments and tasks in the spaces left over in your calendar. This process is referred to as **getting ahead in your calendar.** Always put your personal and lead generation time in your calendar first so that it isn't gobbled up by less important obligations.

Some version of time blocking is done by all successful people. Athletes schedule their workout time, know at what time and for how long they do a specific 'skills' practice, what time they eat, what to eat and how many calories it must be. They cannot and never would miss one of these 'appointments' with themselves. Neither should you.

Sample Weekly Calendar

Mon 3/13	Tue 3/14	Wed 3/15	Thu 3/16	Fri 3/17
8:30 - Prepare for Busine:	8:30 - Prepare for Busine:	8:30 - Prepare for Busine:	8:30 - Prepare for Busine:	8:30 - Prepare for Busine:
9 – 11 Marketing/Business Generation	9 – 11 Marketing/Business Generation	9 – 11 Marketing/Business Generation	9 – 11 Marketing/Business Generation	9 – 11 Marketing/Business Generation
11 – 12p Business Servicing	11 – 12p Business Servicing	11 – 12p Business Servicing	11 – 12p Business Servicing	11 – 12p Business Servicing
12p – 1p Lunch	12p – 1p Lunch	12p – 1p Lunch	12p – 1:45p Lunch w/ Wife	12p – 1p Lunch
1p – 2p Lead Conversion & Follow-Up	1p – 2p Lead Conversion & Follow-Up	1p – 2p Lead Conversion & Follow-Up		1p – 2p Lead Conversion & Follow-Up
2p – 3p Business Servicing	2p – 3p Business Servicing	2p – 3p Business Servicing	2p – 3p Lead Conversion & Follow-Up	2p – 3p Business Servicing
			3p – 4p Business Servicing	
		3:30p – 5p Watch David's T-Ball Game		
4p – 5:30p Listing Presentation - 123 Cottonwood Ct	4p – 6p Show Homes to Johnsons		4:30p – 5:30p Buyer Consultation w/ Taylors	4:30p – 6p Listing Presentation - 456 Spring Creek Way
	6:30p – 8p Family Dinner			6:30p – 8:30p Family Birthday Party

The Erase and Replace Rule

Time management isn't about being a workhorse or burning the midnight oil.

It's more about priorities, planning ahead, and fiercely protecting your time.

However, sometimes an unavoidable crisis will happen that can't be avoided. When this occurs, we apply the Erase and Replace Rule. So let's say a friend needs your help and has asked you to drive him *right now* to the hospital. This time of request is naturally of a last-minute nature! It is on a weekday morning and you want to help him, and you do so. However, you also want to make sure that you keep your marketing department open for 2 hours that morning to not short change yourself on your goal of conducting 500 hours of business generation activities for the year. To remedy this dilemma, you now commit to 3 hours of business generation time in your calendar each of the next two days: You erase your time block on the hospital day and extend your time blocks an hour each on the next two days. Now it's time to put these concepts into action.

1. Use your calendar **to time block your personal commitments and business generation time each morning for the next 3 months.** Remember to honor your calendar and stick to your time blocks!

2. Continue to add 5 new people to your SOI Referral Database per **week** by adding them to your CRM or using the SOI Member Contact Form.

3. Make **5 telephone contacts per day to SOI members** by using any of the scripts provided in our previous training modules.

Whether it's after you first list a seller's home for sale or when you start showing a buyer some properties, **the highest rate of real estate referrals always comes from ongoing working relationships with clients who are engaged somewhere in the process of moving.**

Referrals from existing clients can occur:

1. **Organically** (or naturally), as the client is a natural 'connector' who will deliver referrals to you, without solicitation.

2. Through your **direct ask**, since at certain points in every transaction, you ask the prospect for their referrals.

3. Through **silent expectation and an indirect ask**. You're doing a great job for them, they probably know how to refer you already, and/or you've broached the subject casually.

Options 1 and 3 are the least in our control, as they depend on the client 'just doing it'. Although you never know what type of answer you'll be given when you ask, you have more control with option 2. So the lesson for increasing your number of referrals is: **Always ask. Directly and clearly.**

What Your Clients Are Thinking

'Existing clients' are simply members of your SOI Referral Database right now; they are 'activated' and recipients of your 40 annual contacts. You might think that calling them 'clients' is an exaggeration, since not all SOI members have ever listed or transacted with you yet. However, they know you, what you do and what you offer, and they know your name. They are the most likely individuals around you to be recommending others to you. They do this from one of the strongest places; **they like your service (your email messages, your mailer, how you act when you call them, your events) so much, *they* are choosing to talk about you.**

Just as people becoming aware of a certain make and model of car start to notice that exact vehicle on the road several times a day, **clients preparing to move have a heightened awareness of other people looking to do the same.** This is their day-to-day focus, the recurring subject of their conversations, it is one of their new habits. Consider someone going on vacation to Hawaii. What's the main topic of their conversations with friends, family, co-workers – really anyone they come in contact with? Hawaii, of course.

This commonality with others often dictates many of their social and professional conversations, which puts your chances of receiving real estate referrals at an all-time high.

Organized Referral Process

Every time you remind your clients during a transaction that you *work by referral*, you increase the likelihood of receiving real estate referrals.

Agents who systematize their referral process increase the number of referrals received by training clients on how to refer them. Finally, you carefully script your requests. How you ask for a referral can be as impactful as *how often* or *when*.

Organized Referral Process:

1. **Remind the Client** ("You know that I work by referrals")
2. **Train the Client** ("Who do you know that is thinking about moving?")
3. **Script the Ask** (See next section)
4. **Repeat steps 1-3**

This is why top agents will **ask early and often** in a systematic fashion throughout each transaction and at each new contact, and this becomes their Organized Referral Process. Numerous reminders to ask for real estate referrals become a part of their Listing-to-Contract and Contract-to-Closing checklists. This ensures that they always bring up the topic.

While the life of the contract is a crucial time to prospect for referrals, it's just as crucial to outline expectations after the contract is satisfied. Having an 'agent for life' mentality starts with having a schedule of what that looks like for both you and the client, and a script. By having this laid out ahead of time, your scripts will follow a timeline that occurs intentionally, rather than by happenstance.

Scripted Asks

The key then becomes familiarizing yourself with tested real estate scripts that you are comfortable with. We've already proposed a number of scripts to you, and this is for one reason: They work.

Most agents shy away from the use of real estate scripts for fear of sounding too pushy or too 'canned'. However, effective real estate scripts should never come off like a sales pitch, instead feel comfortable and conversational as you master them. Asking your clients for referrals throughout their transactions should just roll off the tongue confidently and naturally.

When it comes to scripts and referrals, play close attention to what's holding you back from asking for the referral: You don't want to appear to be 'desperate' for new business; you don't want to make it seem that business is bad for you right now. Avoiding this impression means you come from confidence and a relaxed posture, and remain conversational. Practice one of these Scripts to build your confidence:

- "By the way, the majority of my business comes by word-of-mouth from past clients. It's how I prefer to run my business. So, if you know anyone that is looking to buy or sell a home this year, would you mind referring them to me?"

- "I want to work with more clients like you, and I find that people looking to move know others in the same position. How would you feel about referring my services to them?"

- "It's been really great working with you thus far, and I feel really grateful to Jane for introducing you to me. If it wasn't for her, I would've never met you. So, I just wanted to take the time to ask you if you know anyone else that is looking to buy or sell a home, and if you would feel comfortable introducing them to me?"

- "Who else do you know that needs to move right now?"

- "You are so great to work with, and I find that people typically hang around similar people. I would love to work with more people like you, so do you know anyone looking to move in the near future?"

- "Who do you know that I should know?"

- "Because you are in the process of moving right now, you will overhear a lot of conversations from different people looking to move when you are out and about. When you do, would you mind giving them my phone number and ask them to call me?"

Look at table turnover in restaurants – a diner leaves, and the owner would love to fill that table again right away. It keeps him busy, prosperous and means that his food and prices and atmosphere are attractive. Also, the fact that the restaurant is full at lunch or dinner time when you look in its window is a sort of 'referral' that the food is good.

When your current client closes on their sale or their purchase, they're also creating an 'empty table' for a new current client; from your perspective as a business owner, a glowing recommendation/referral can also ease nervous or unsure clients through this familiar connection. Every satisfied client can become a lead generator on your team – and they will, as you **remind them, train them, and script your ask.**

Train the Client

Systemization through scripts, scheduling and habit is crucial since it holds agents accountable to asking for referrals with greater frequency.

Training your clients at each conversation is the top way to elicit referrals.

The following are times you might have lost the chance to train your clients about **who represents a great referral for you:**

- Was the existing client **aware of what types of referrals** you were asking for? Don't lose a *condo* referral because your clients think you only work with homes. Let clients know your range of action includes businesses for sale, land, commercial buildings, condos, multifamily properties ... as appropriate.

- Was the client **aware of *where* to look for referrals on your behalf?** You need to train them to think of all their own sphere of influence, their connections and networks. You ask them who they know at work, among their friends, within their family or immediate neighbors, in their sports and hobby clubs, etc.

- Was there a **specific service you provided** this client that would prompt you to ask for a referral – **and you did not?** Highlight their own transaction as something their own sphere of influence might be searching for. You say, "We just got you into a great new financing program! Who else can you think of who needs to consider refinancing, too?"

- Was there a previous referral made by this SOI member, and **he didn't receive your follow-up or thanks?** Shame on you! That is not only a client who will never become your repeat client, but someone who will never, ever refer anyone to you! Fix this with a new, automated thank-you process that is part of every transaction checklist.

- What was your **method of contact?** Face-to-face appointment or lunch, phone, text messages might all carry more weight with clients – due to their directness – than emails or mailers. Be in direct touch.

Closing Time

Just because an SOI member has closed one transaction with you never, ever, ever means you remove him from your SOI Database! You keep sending your client – still a respected SOI member in your Referral Database – the 40 contacts per year!

Average agents 'take the commission check and run' after a transaction closes, and will rarely follow up with their clients to ask how things are going. They lose out on countless referrals, because they have cut off the people they ask!

*After transactions close, staying in touch with clients provides an amazing way to blend your marketing activities with customer service ... **and earn even more referrals.***

Top producers know that following up with clients after closing provides increased opportunities to 'touch' their clients several more times than just the scheduled 40 and that these 'bonus contacts' can boost their chances of receiving referral business. During these post-transaction contacts, your happy client might hear of someone looking to invest, buy or sell houses, condos, or land, and he will think of you.

Add Value, Gain Referrals

There are many opportunities to create value for clients after – even years after – a closed transaction with them.

You will never know if he is in the market for a long-term investment such as a single condo, a vacation home, or a small multifamily property unless you are in regular contact through your phone calls, and other Contact Plan means. You will never know if he is desperately looking for a reputable ___ (Fill in the blank with any of the professions which are part of your Preferred Vendor List) unless you ask him ... and have sent him your updates to the List as you create them. You'll never know that his recently graduated child is in the market for a small house in her parents' neighborhood ... unless you remain in touch, and **ask.**

Every touch is a reminder of their great experience with you and your service as a real estate agent.

PAST CLIENT FOLLOW-UP SCRIPT

30, 90, 180 Days After Closing

"Hi _____, it's Annie Agent with ABC Real Estate. I'm just calling to check in with you to see how you're doing in your new home!

"How has your new home been treating you?" (Remember that the key is to continue to ask questions to uncover a need that you can help with.)

"I remember some things you wanted to change. What have you done to it so far?"

"Great! What work or improvements are you planning in the future? Okay, that sounds interesting! Would it help if we gave you the contact information of some professionals that we trust that could help you get that done at a reasonable cost?"

"Great! I'm glad our Preferred Vendor List was of help to you when you did that remodeling. Well, don't forget that Vendor List. And if you come across a great provider that is not on my list, would you please call me with their name and number?"

"You see, we want you to think of us as your total home resource. You can save yourself some time & frustration by letting us refer you to a tested and trusted company for any home ownership needs that may come up. Would that benefit you?"

"Great? *As you know, most of my business comes by word of mouth from my clients.* So, with that said, do you know anyone else looking to move in the near future?"

ACTION STEPS:

1. **Script Modification**: Imagine how you would modify the above script to chat about their refinancing needs...search for investment properties...getting an adult child/other referred person qualified for a mortgage or into a new property search with you...providing them a new service of yours? Remember to close each script with an **ask for a referral, and prompt them on who makes a referral for you.**

2. **Referral Checks**: Now list the phone contacts you have scheduled with your current clients, and match them up with a script such as you devised in #1. **These represent chances to directly ask for referrals and train clients on who makes a great referral for you ... while you provide a needed service to them.**

3. **Post-Transaction Plan**: Now merge post-transaction contacts and conversations with clients into your SOI Contact Plan.

4. **Contact Past Clients**: Now call all clients whom you have not contacted in their post-transaction period of the past year, and re-engage with them. **Ask directly for referrals. Train and prompt them on who makes a referral for you.**

Staying on track with your Database Contact Plan is no simple task. Just because you know what you need to do to keep up with your contacts and are protecting the time to do it **doesn't mean you are actually getting it done.** Because of this risk, it is crucial to track your business generation activities.

Your tracking indicators have a direct impact on your **time** (its usage and management), **money** (how much income you are losing out on by not following through with your SOI Contact Plan or the development of your SOI database), and your **state of mind** (in a prior module, we discussed the risks involved in not nipping your **resistance** to making consistent and scheduled SOI contacts in the bud).

As a business owner, you are responsible for

1. efforts going into the business that build its reputation and promote its growth

2. measuring the effectiveness of those efforts – the number of closed transactions is one metric of effectiveness, and there are a number of others

3. fixing/changing what is not producing the expected number (or more) closed transactions.

You will need to have tools for measuring your results and outcomes – but also have a personal willingness to change how you are doing things when poor or no results are forthcoming. Let's say you are finding that you:

• Make lots of calls, yet have no appointments.

How to remedy that? Make more calls, adjust what you're saying, or ...?

• Have 8 appointments, but take 1 listing.

How do you improve this ratio of appointments-to-listings? Define if it really was an appointment, practice/change your presentation, or ...?

• Have 13 listings, only 2 of them with showings.

What's preventing the conversions? The cost of this outcome to my bottom line is ...?

*What you need to establish is some **KPI**: some **Key Performance Indicators***

KPIs

Shift your perspective a bit and consider this: If one's book of business hasn't improved for 5 years, has it really been 5 years of great business, or the same lackluster year repeated 5 times? Only performance metrics or KPI can tell you.

A salesperson employed in a larger corporation can look at a level of activity, and deduce success or failure – often in relation to his own past results or the results of higher/lower-producing salespeople he works with. You are not in that case, so you need other means of measuring performance.

The need for tracking is real, whether your numbers are outstanding or disastrously bad. As a business owner, you have the task of tracking the real story, the reasons for the outcomes you have. If you have the recipe for achieving outstanding results, but don't know how you have 'achieved' the disastrous results you see, you haven't done your job. It is the recipe for changing bad results to great ones that you need to find!

Your Database Contact Plan will put you ahead of your competition when you work it consistently – it means you're treating all aspects of your business with the same planning, attention and commitment. Too many businesses treat referrals and recommendations from their SOI as a bonus or as a passive source of business – you, however, know from studying all the modules to date, that it takes well-planned action to *earn* those referrals.

What are your best KPI? There are dozens, but you probably need only a handful – and you have seen a number of them in prior modules. We simply have not called them KPIs until now. Here for memory are your two primary KPI:

1. **40 Contacts/Member/Year** - At least 3 types of touches, for a total of 40 touches per year.

2. **7-to-1** - 40 annual contacts per member will result in 1 closed transaction for every 7 people in your SOI Referral Database. It is, of course, the closed transaction that pays you your commission.

Here are **other Key Performance Indicators** for you to consider actively, or at least periodically, tracking:

- 40 Annual Contacts, including as a 'Basic Contact Plan' 26 emails (one every 2 weeks), 12 mailers (sent once a month) and 2 phone calls (made once every 6 months).

- Track the 7-to-1 ratio results.

- Beyond the Basic Contact Plan, you add Drop-by visits, Face-to-face visits, Facebook Friend messages (who become SOI members and benefit from your automated contacts), Other social media followers/friends, Client appreciation events, Delivery of hand-written notes

- Never eliminating an individual who knows you by name from your SOI except at their express request; adding new people weekly to your SOI database - they are eligible for the database when they know who you are by name.

- SOI Database maintenance (updates to contact information of SOI members each time you are in touch with them) or scrubbing it on a predetermined schedule.

- Always asking for referrals, whether you are emailing, calling or face-to-face.

- Using Scripts until you have them memorized.

- Build a Preferred Vendor List as part of your give-and-give Referral Networking. These are business owners or professionals whom you may recommend to your SOI members, and whom you can exchange referrals. Always ask for a referral.

- Full and consistent usage of your chosen CRM.

- Track the conversion of leads from contact to an inperson buyer consultation appointment.

- Track the number of times you propose a new SOI member for MLS.

- Track the number of times you deliver a pre-listing packet.

- Observe your comfort or discomfort in fielding buyer/seller objections and questions.

- The number of hours spent weekly in business-building activities.

- Your ability to let incoming calls go to voicemail or to short-circuit interruptions while you complete your Contact Plan schedule.

- Track the value of your Social Media outreach.

How Does the KPI 'Work'?

How to use a KPI is easily demonstrated with our first metric, the **40 contacts:**

1. The KPI is **"Make 40 Contacts/Member/Year."** That is the 'performance measure' *minimum* that you must achieve to get the results we have explained in prior modules.

2. **If you fall short of the 40 contacts in a year's time, you have not achieved that KPI goal, plain and simple.** Not

doing so, as we have explained, puts your gross commission income at risk, since everything depends on those 40 contacts being made.

3. Next, you ask, **"Why didn't I?"**

a) If the answer is that you've failed to fully set up your email messages and properly schedule (automate) them – you know that is a clear thing to fix.

b) If the answer is that you procrastinated about making those phone calls, you know that you need some help being accountable to that schedule of calls (or that you need to actually put them in your agenda because now you see how important that tactic really is).

c) If the answer is that you didn't 'feel like' spending the cash on mailers, well – do you now see how it has affected your business performance and resulted in fewer closed transactions?

That is a KPI's strength – determining the expected result, and showing you inirrefutable numbers that

1) you have succeeded or 2) that you have failed.

Never Too Late

If you have been paying attention to prior modules, you have very likely already started to make the adjustments to your business development approach with our suggestions. You have become more intentional about how you spend your time and where you focus your activities. Hopefully you have already set up CRM or other tracking systems, but if not – do it now. It is never too late.

Keeping track of which activities you perform to develop your SOI database and grow your business's results is vital to success. Go back into all earlier modules to lift out all the KPI that we have presented. It is not just busy-work! These are vital measures of future success. Following our KPIs will determine how 'big' you succeed or fail in real estate.

Tracking Infuses Accountability

Another perspective on tracking results is to look at the percentage of time you spend doing tasks or activities. The **10-10-80 principle** can help break it down:

- **10%:** Spend 10% of your time learning what to do – educating yourself. That is what you are doing with this book. Periodically, you take up a new course or book that helps you keep current on trends in this industry or helps you improve in areas you've identified as weak.

- **10%:** Spend 10% of your time to simply launch – start doing the activities or tasks we have presented in this book. This includes the set-up time for your CRM, drafting its automated email messages and scheduling them, drafting and automating your mailers with a postal service and so on. Then, the following year, you polish up or revise the content of those messages and re-automate the send.

- **80%:** Spend 80% of your time Just Doing It, as the Nike sport shoe people have been saying for years – and keep doing the right business-building activities day by day. You stay in touch with and grow your SOI database according to your Contact Plan, getting more comfortable and more skilled at it as you 'improve by doing'.

The 80% of Just Doing It will energize you and your business, but only if your preparation time has included those two 10% efforts.

1. **Success:** It worked, business was generated, and so you repeat the process.

2. **Commitment:** You've given your word to an accountability partner, an SOI member, a family member overtly or silently – and you follow through.

3. **Mastery:** The adrenaline rush of now being great at something through experience or through a greater comfort doing formerly uncomfortable tasks – like phone calls or knock-on-door-with-flyers – leads you to look forward to doing it for the results you derive from them.

4. **Purpose:** The end result of following your Contact Plan and recording your results – new referrals for the SOI database, a new seller listing, several new confirmed buyer decisions at once – proves out that your determination to stick to the Plan and be accountable to its steps pays off. Seeing annual and quarterly results sky-rocket can be a large motivator. But when you have daily and weekly business-building outcomes, you are truly pumped to do what has obviously worked – and do it consistently.

Tracking Creates Clarity

The **#5 reason accountability works** needs a section all of its own. It is the **Clarity** it provides to you. Your KPI and all other numbers and activities you decide are important to track have a way of jolting you into fully alert awareness. The KPI reveal perhaps a new, highly effective strategy that you need to keep doing; they show that an activity we spend hours a week performing is non-productive of a single desired result. Act on what is clearly before your eyes!

The SOI Contact Plan is a tool that keeps you focused on doing proven activities, so that you don't get caught up in bemoaning results (or lack of them):

- Agent Arthur makes the requisite 20 daily telephone client database contacts with no thought of whether the calls 'are worth it or not'. He may feel a sense of accomplishment if the focus was **completing that task** of reaching out a few times a year to keep the stream of communication open, while prospecting for referrals.

- Agent Andrew, who focuses solely on results in his mind, may experience only depression if he made the 20 calls but received no leads from them right away. His mindset doesn't allow him to assign a proper importance to the **touch** and its performance over time.

You are playing a number game. A game of touches. A knowledgeable agent understands this and knows that eventually the leads and appointments will come so long as the activity persists. **You have**

total control of the effort and limited control over the outcome, so your job is to improve your performance on the effort – making sure tasks and activities are performed consistently.

Tracking Helps You Test

We have spoken about how having a scorecard of activity which you update daily, weekly, or monthly allows you to see how you are doing in relation to your KPIs. It shows you seasonal and other types of trends in your marketplace and among your SOI.

Tracking allows you to notice that you need to dial 60 times to reach 20 SOI contacts in the early morning. You do this 5 days each week, and thus track 300 attempted calls for 100 touches.

- The next week, they had made their contacts during the evening on two of the days, and tracked 30 calls to find 20 contacts.

- Week 3, they sent out a text before calling, and tracked 25 calls: 20 contacts.

Let's take a look at what their tracking scoreboard would look like:

5-day Week	AM Calls	PM Calls	Live Contacts	Total Calls	Calls Made / Live Contacts
Week 1	300	0	100	300	3:1
Week 2	180	60	100	240	2.4:1
Week 3	180	50	100	125	1.25:1

Such an exercise in tracking allows you to determine the most profitable and results-producing time to make your phone calls. Thus, you stick to morning calling as your touches are highest at that time of day. And you are comforted that time usage is returning the best results.

Here is another example of what you may track and how you might do it.

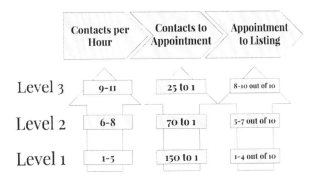

	Contacts per Hour	Contacts to Appointment	Appointment to Listing
Level 3	9-11	25 to 1	8-10 out of 10
Level 2	6-8	70 to 1	5-7 out of 10
Level 1	1-5	150 to 1	1-4 out of 10

Jack Roberts at ABC Realty helped us find our current home 3 years ago. Amazingly, he has kept in touch and when our son was looking for a condo, Jack was right there to guide him through the whole process. Painless! We trust Jack – he's like a member of the family.

As you look at a Level 1 tracking, you see a 10-40% appointment to listing outcome. Not bad, you think? Perhaps, but only until you look at your outcome in a Level 3, where you have achieved an 80-100% rate of success.

If your KPI tracking shows a Level 1 outcome, here are questions you ask. And ask you must, in order to properly troubleshoot the 'problem' of a 'low' 10-40% appointment to listing outcome.

Helpful questions to analyze your approach:

1. What steps could I take to increase contacts per hour?
2. Is my call list prepared in advance of my daily calling session, or is it hunt-and-find? Change this as needed.
3. Are interruptions in my daily calling session my problem? Try tracking each one.
4. How much time is spent recording notes from contacts? Could I do it as I speak?
5. Am I fluctuating call session times to reach more contacts?
6. Am I contacting the person too frequently, to avoid longer 'catch-up' calls? Stop.
7. Am I following a script? Start.
8. Am I leaving voicemails? Stop.
9. To improve contact-to-appointment ratio, what will give me a template for better success? Perhaps start systematically offering an appointment during calls.

10. Am I employing different scripts to set appointments? Choose one and master it.

11. Do they have enough trust in me to hear more? Why not? What must I change to gain sincere trust?

12. Have I shared what an appointment will look like, and how long it will take?

13. To improve appointment-to-listing ratio, what will move the needle up?

14. Could I practice my presentation more?

15. Could I employ different campaigns to cause risk to go down?

16. Could I field questions or handle the objections in a different way?

17. Am I using trial closes, and asking for the contract?

The Essential Analysis

What we have presented above are questions that help you analyze what you are doing well and what can be changed for better outcomes. How you track it is not that important, but write it out in a way that works for you. While tracking software exists for CRMs, but you can simply also track such tests with pen-and-paper, a simple Excel worksheet, or a whiteboard.

Keep in mind, however, that no amount of tracking is worth your time if you don't review it and make a rational decision supported by a plan. The plan may simply be 'schedule all my calling before 11 am from now on', but you know *why* you are doing so – your tracking has proven its effectiveness.

Tracking and doing such comparative tests helps you see where your attempts are missing the mark. It might be that you need training or confidence in performing the activity.

If tracking and meeting (or not) your predetermined KPI shows you need to improve your people skills, look for a course and take it. Many an agent has discovered that he is not 'a natural', doesn't have a 'gift of the gab' or doesn't have a clue how to gain and keep control of a conversation. Don't despair. If you need to *learn* ways to verbally break the ice in a door-knocking activity, or in opening or controlling a phone conversation or appointment dialog – do it – practice, learn, grow your confidence!

Remember that most agents will not be consistent, scheduled and regular in contacting their SOI and in even having a 40-contact-per-year approach. You have a leg up on these other local agents, but only if you plan your contacts and work your plan. **Having a set number of KPI such as we have presented is your 'competitive advantage'.**

Other agents guess or speculate as to the results they'll have at year end. You know what to expect. You have set goals that we call KPI, which in turn direct all your daily activities, and those in turn give you a more predictable outcome than other agents could hope for.

Never Underestimate the SOI Contact Plan

We have been saying it in many ways:

If agents do the tracking and trace the source of *closed transactions* regularly, they always find that the largest percentage comes from their *regular SOI contacts*, and *referrals from their SOI members.*

For additional thoughts on tracking, watch these videos **and take notes as you view:**

How to Generate Business without a Client Database
VIDEO: https://youtu.be/uqLb0PaIuQY

Tracking Real Estate Conversion Ratios
VIDEO: https://youtu.be/5HA9p6Dngmo

Prospecting Conversion Rates for Real Estate Agents
VIDEO: https://youtu.be/GDIjKr2zX-4

ACTION STEPS:

1. **Use the Daily SOI Contact** Form to track the telephone contacts you make to your SOI.

2. **Schedule Your Tracking and Analytical Time**

   a) Complete your tracking sheet or scorecard daily, filling it out as you go along. This prevents 'trying to remember' at day's end, or not doing it at all.

   a) Schedule a weekly 30-minute appointment with yourself to review and break down the meaning of your numbers. If you have staff, a coach, or a business partner, this can be an 'accountability meeting' with staff, since more eyes can see more details. Alternatively, schedule a quiet time just for you to look at and read the message in your numbers.

3. **Review the 5 Reasons Accountability Works:** When you are lost, spinning your wheels, procrastinating or resisting working your Contact Plan, review these great reasons to dig in.

4. **Review your Level:** Determine your level of lead generation based on the chart given; Level 3, 2, or 1. Ask questions of yourself to honestly decide on a course of action to improve things. **Then follow your new approach.**

5. **Write the KPI that are particularly important to you in your business.** Track them. Review and analyze them. Ask questions of yourself to honestly decide on a course of action to improve things. **Then follow your new approach.**

Home and condo owners across the country are quite accustomed to those Open House signs that point the way to a neighbor's home on the weekends. Open Houses overtly serve to more quickly sell a property, but the Open House event, well marketed and operated:

1. **Helps to sell the home more quickly** – Neighbors, friends, family members, anyone who's responding to your marketing or invitations, will get the showroom experience on Open House Day. They can walk into the home and see how it matches their needs or wants. While many efforts of the real estate agent may be foreign or unknown to the general public, the Open House is a familiar, convenient, and comfortable way to not only view more homes, but choose their next one.

2. **Shows your seller/client you are proactively marketing the home:** A well-attended, well-promoted Open House shows the seller that not only do you take action, your actions yield results in the one medium any homeowner can understand – a crowd of curious, potential buyers.

Why Focus on Listings and Open Houses?

Listings combined with one or two immediate Open House events can result in a number of other, **business-building benefits for you.**

Leads galore. Those who have the listings control the leads. Buyers are like bumble bees. If you want to catch a bumble bee, you don't go chasing it all over town. That would take too much time (commute time), you wouldn't likely ever catch it (conversion), and you might even end up getting stung (not a lead, but a tire-kicker). **A smarter approach might be to control the supply of flowers (listings) that attracts bumblebees.** Listings attract buyers when you are intentional about your capture systems.

During an Open House, you grow your Sphere of Influence (SOI) Referral Database as you meet guests. The opportunity of walking through a home on the market can attract new faces, neighbors and other locals who might not respond to direct mail or prospecting. The Open House affords you the opportunity to start or build a relationship in person, in exchange for a viewing of the home you're promoting.

An Open House allows you to meet and secure buyers as clients who are looking at homes. A percentage of guests who are in the market to buy a home may not be represented by an agent, or only informally. The Open House yields buyer connections for you, while the prospective buyer gets to see you in action.

An Open House introduces you to neighbors and opens the door to getting their listings – People looking to sell within the year often start looking at Open Houses in their neighborhood to size up the competition and determine the price at which they might be able to sell. They also frequently size you up as a potential agent to list their home, looking at crowd size, marketing materials provided, signage, and your own personal presentation as a professional.

You have a more rational time management, since you can manage 4 listings in the time it takes to handle one active buyer. This is why most top producing agents have the most listings, while most burned-out agents focus on representing buyers. Buyer agents typically have to work evenings and weekends when their clients are off work and able to look at homes. Once a property is listed, listing agents now leverage every buyer agent's time in the market's database by putting the sign in the yard and putting the property on the Multiple Listing Service.

You develop your brand and name recognition, as other sellers in the immediate neighborhood see the listing agent's signs and marketing activities around them. This exposure makes you a household name in most neighborhoods just from signage exposure alone, but also from your knock-on-doors and flyer delivery efforts. People love to call on a familiar face when it comes time to list their property or go in search of a new home for themselves. You have already built up a respectable amount of goodwill, so they are likely to come to you.

Having a listing-focus matching your Open House efforts is vital.

The Where and When of an Open House

Choosing where and when to host an Open House is your initial step – and keep in mind that you won't hold an Open House on every listed property, or hold it in the same way from one property type to another. A farmhouse on 30 acres, a 10th floor condo in a high-security building, a luxury home with millions of dollars of designer furniture, artwork, and priceless sport car collections – these types of property require different strategies from those we cover here. Yet this is where some agents are finding opportunity because their competition declined to compete. Let's cover fundamentals, and you'll be unlimited with where you go from there.

Where

Having a specific purpose for your Open House is going to sway some of the factors on where you choose to host your Open House; yet first you need a choice of listings. Some agents would consider that if they have 1 listing, that's where they'll be spending their Saturdays or Sundays. If it shows the seller you are proactive, helps to sell the home, attracts people for your SOI Referral Database, and finds buyers for the home – you hold the Open House.

However, look at local environment and conditions which may decide you **against** an Open House:

- very little to no road traffic
- prohibitive association rules (condo's; subdivisions with HOAs, etc.)
- access issues due to security
- access issues due to limited parking
- danger of any kind to property or people
- condition of the house won't show well in an Open House setting
- too many other listings in the neighborhood that day (this has pro's and con's)

Consider these factors as well:

What's the market like in this price range? A sluggish market may mean no guests. What's the annual turnover rate in the neighborhood for the last 12 months – how many homes have sold in this neighborhood, and how many have been listed versus how many 'doors' there are?

What are local amenities, businesses and such? Depending on the day of the week you host your Open House, community events that draw crowds, like races, farmer's markets, or church services could increase how many people attend.

What has previous Open House attendance looked like? Find out why it was that good or that bad.

When

Get the Open House set up and scheduled at the moment when the listing agreement is signed. Time really is of the essence when scheduling an Open House, especially in a red-hot market. It is crucial to schedule one or even two Open Houses during your initial listing consultation. Preferably, those two Open Houses can be held over the next one or two weekends.

But when to schedule it? The time of day and the day of the week you hold your Open House should start with you. While this feels like a broad answer, the best time is the time where traffic, promotion, and presentation all collide, as it were, at their highest points.

Decide on late mornings, afternoons or evenings – or a mix of all three. Decide on how long you'll hold the home open: Typically, it will be open for 2-5 hours, weekday or weekend. See the 'Script – Scheduling an Open House' at the end of this module.

Marketing Open Houses

To achieve a massive flow of qualified (home buyers) guest traffic to your Open House, you must promote heavily before the Open House date – there is no secret.

Marketing tactics should be diversified, as you test a blend of flyers or direct mailers to your SOI and the neighbors, MLS Open House listing, emails, door hangers and knock-on-doors campaign, local posters and signs, sandwich Open House signage, social media announcement, etc.

Always welcome the local neighbors to your Open Houses without pre-judgment about them just being tire-kickers – get them into your SOI Referral Database. They could turn into buyers or sellers – or know other buyers or sellers right now – so you start

developing that name-recognition relationship (Remembers: your SOI are people who know who you are and remember your name) at the Open House itself.

Make sure your marketing materials are clear about your purpose. Neighbors should know that they're being contacted about the Open House because of our knowledge that **"the ultimate purchaser of a home is often a friend, family member or acquaintance of someone that already lives in the neighborhood."** Emphasize the connection between existing residents and a home's ultimate buyer during door knocking and circle prospecting. Knock-on-doors to deliver a flyer makes another great method for marketing Open Houses. If you take that approach, you knock on the doors of homes in the neighborhood about one week before the Open House.

Along with flyers, you can also market your Open House by using auto-dialers. With an auto-dialer, you'll be able to automatically call the entire neighborhood with automated calls. Auto-dialers often have a feature that lets you create a prerecorded message and leave it whenever you hit a neighbor's voicemail. Your message can advertise the local Open House, encourage 'neighbors welcome', give the address clearly two times, and explain that all neighbors are encouraged to attend – "because you might be or know the future owner of this beautiful home!".

Open Houses can also be a fantastic time to connect with your Preferred Vendors and other members of your Referral Network. Invite them to the Open House and invite them to encourage traffic to it from their own network. This allows them to see the type and caliber of properties your clients are buying/selling and creates a picture in their minds about new ways they can offer their services to your SOI Database – through you.

Another point on Open Houses – you can still hold them *even if a home goes under contract* beforehand. Notice that we're talking about 'under contract' as opposed to 'sold'. A status of 'sold' deprives you of all the Open House opportunities. Having a property 'under contract' doesn't preclude the Open House.

Open House Signage

Agents who focus on listings differ on the way they use Open House signs. Traditional agents believe they're holding the Open House to find buyers. So, the traditional agent places signs for the event on major thoroughfares *outside the neighborhood.* They do this in the hope of luring people into the neighborhood to see the Open House.

This traditional method largely fails to attract lots of traffic, because it doesn't attract new buyers to the home that weren't already attempting to find it anyway. The signs only help people who were already coming to look at it find the house.

Top agents know to place their Open House signs generously *within* the neighborhood, not just on the route *to* the neighborhood. This way every resident of the neighborhood will know that this local house is open. Indeed, no neighbor leaving or entering the neighborhood can miss the fact that a neighboring home is an Open House by that agent. And, as we have said, the agent welcomes all guests – all neighbors – to view the property.

Open House Guest List/Registration

Your Open House must also have a guest list for visitors to sign. The Open House guest list should always ask for:

> Guest's name
>
> Physical address
>
> Phone number
>
> Email address

Make sure the guest list is placed somewhere in the center of the home, a place where you'll be primarily located. A guest list gives you complete contact information for each neighbor as he comes through the home. As you might expect, this information enables you to enter these individuals into your SOI Contact Database and send Open House attendees marketing material for properties in the future. The guest list makes a great way to build your database in a given neighborhood.

Guest lists help you, but what's in it for the visitor? Why would they willingly give out personal information – especially if they're wanting to see the house without feeling any pressure? See the 'Script – Promoting Your Open House' later in this module, as well as the Scripts on 'Security' and 'Insurance' below.

Security? Insurance? Neither is an exaggeration. Understand that, sadly, Open Houses have been the opening for many burglaries. Can any burglar imagine a better opportunity to actually be invited in 'to case the joint' than a publicized Open House? Protect your seller's interests!

As for insurance, it's likewise a real concern. This is because damage or personal injury could occur during the Open House on the property. In fact, a great point to mention during your listing presentation is to have the owners check with their insurance provider about coverage while being on the market. Pair this with your mention of Home Warranties and you'll have covered all your bases. If anything unfortunate did happen, it could potentially render your business responsible for damages. Protect your own business's interests!

With all this talk about insurance and security, don't lose sight of the other very important reason for guest lists. **Guest lists build your database.** Keep that in mind, even amid the other reasons. Nonetheless, you're ultimately seeking more than just a 'pile of names'. **You want conversations and those lead to conversions.**

During the Open House

During the Open House, always stay active and engaged. Interacting with your guests is a crucial balance between service and shadowing; lean towards the former. Whether guests prefer a self-guided tour or not, know the house and property in order to answer questions. **Unanswered questions mean that you are not really interested in selling this property and you will lose opportunities.**

Any of the following questions might be good lead-ins to gaining a new buyer, a new listing or more information about properties in the area:

- Do you live in the area?
- Are you currently a home owner?
- Have you gone to many Open Houses?
- Is there an area that you are particularly interested in?
- Have you been looking around a lot?
- What price range are you looking at?
- Are you currently working with an agent?
- What is your time frame for making a decision?

SCRIPT - SCHEDULING AN OPEN HOUSE

"Mr./Mrs. SELLER, we find that the vast majority of homes that sell at a price close to our listing price sell within the first few weeks of putting the home up for sale in the market.

Accordingly, we have great success when we generate multiple offers from different buyers at the same time. More often than not, this occurs within the first couple weeks of putting a home up for sale. This is why we market so hard through mail, flyers, telephone calls, and hold Open Houses right at the time of listing.

We have also seen success at generating prices above or at the asking price when we can create multiple offer situations. Further, if your home does go under contract or at least generates an offer prior to holding the Open House – nothing is more effective at keeping that buyer honest than holding an Open House as scheduled previously. For example, if we are negotiating back and forth with different offers – it often takes many days, if not a week. If, during this process, we hold a pre-scheduled Open House at the home, we can create extreme urgency with the potential buyer that's in negotiations with us.

When a home is under contract or at least being negotiated, buyers drive by the home to show it to friends and family members – as their future home. And there is nothing worse than seeing people walk through it who may steal it away. This strikes fear in the heart of the buyer and favors you the seller.

Further, in situations where an offer has already been negotiated and accepted, holding pre-set Open Houses helps show buyers that other people are interested in the home. This way when it comes time to inspect and negotiate improvements in the home, later in the transaction process, the buyer will be less picky. And that, once again, strengthens the buying and negotiating power of you, the seller."

SCRIPT – PROMOTING YOUR OPEN HOUSE

"Hi, I'm John Smith with ABC Realty. We have your neighbor's home at 123 Main Street up for sale and we are holding a special Open House on Saturday from 11:00am to 3:00pm. **Since we know that the ultimate purchaser of a home is often a friend, family member or acquaintance of someone that already lives in the same neighborhood, we are inviting the entire neighborhood to come by to take a look.** If you happen to know or meet someone looking to move into your community, this is a great way for you to hand-pick pick your own neighbors! Do you think you can swing by?"

[Wait for response and proceed with . . .]

[If Yes]: "Great! And since we are doing everything we can to get your neighbor's home sold, I promised my seller that I'd ask: Do you know anyone looking to buy or sell a home in the area?"

[If No]: "No problem, I totally understand. And since we are doing everything we can to get your neighbor's home sold, I promised my seller that I'd ask: Do you know anyone looking to buy or sell a home in the near future?"

[Ask for a Pre-Listing Appointment]

Possible Follow Up Question]: "And by the way, it's my intent to focus my practice in this neighborhood. So I'm providing all of the homeowners a complimentary value of $500 with the hope that they might consider interviewing me when and if they ever decide to sell their home in the future. You see, an appraiser would typically charge you around $500 to appraise your home, and I'm attempting to help you alleviate that cost to determine what your home would be worth in this market. Would knowing your home's current value be of any benefit to you?"

[If they are hesitant or otherwise object, proceed with . . .]

[Objection Handler] "I see, and I want to assure you that

there would be absolutely no obligation on your part. Again, this is a courtesy service that I am providing free of charge to all your neighbors with the hope that if you decided to sell 5, 10 or 20 years down the road, you would consider *interviewing me for the job*.

I would also never want you to straighten up your home just for me. I'm a REALTOR® and we're very used to viewing homes long before they're ready to show. I assure you it won't affect the value at all, and I'll be in and out in minutes. How does that sound?"

[If they are interested proceed with . . .]

[If Yes]: "Great! Would 3:00 or 5:00 tomorrow work better for you?"

[Also be sure to obtain all of their contact information so that you can add them to your SOI Referral Database to stay in touch with them over time.]

[If No]: "No problem – consider this a standing offer and feel free to contact me if you are ever curious about your home's current value. In the meantime, can I count on you to let me know if you bump into anyone looking to move into the area so that we can get your neighbor's home sold?"

[Wait for a response] "Great! I truly appreciate your time and help."

OPEN HOUSE SCRIPT #1 - "SECURITY"

"Thanks for signing in – it is for security purposes. I need to keep a record of everyone that comes through the house."

[Hold the paper Open House flyer for the property as they complete the guest list, and then provide it to them once they are done.]

OPEN HOUSE SCRIPT #2 - "INSURANCE"

"Thanks for signing in for insurance purposes. I have to keep a log of every guest that walks through the home."

[Hold the paper Open House flyer for the property as they complete the guest list, and then provide it to them once they are done.]

FOLLOW-UP SCRIPT FOR POTENTIAL **BUYERS:**

A. "You know, trying to find a house looking at Open Houses is very difficult. Only a very small percentage of homes are open at any given time, so what you're looking at is just the tip of the iceberg."

Then follow by suggesting one of the following:

- Suggest setting appointments to show other homes for sale in the area
- Use computer to access MLS online to select homes that fit their criteria and set appointments to show all of them in one day/time; and/or
- Use computer to access MLS online to get contact information and start them on client auto-prospecting
- Set an appointment at the office to meet

FOLLOW-UP SCRIPT & DIALOGUE - NEIGHBORS/ SELLERS

"If you don't mind, it would greatly help me if I could get some marketing feedback from you. Did you happen to see the flyer I created for this home with the Comparative Market Analysis (CMA) on the back?

"Great! I'm curious if this was of any benefit to you. You see, I was attempting to show you the sizes and prices of other homes in the area so that you could use the neighborhood's average price per square foot to get a rough idea of what your house is worth in this market. Do you happen to know the square footage of your home?

"Terrific! Thank you. Now often times your home will have different amenities and features than the houses listed on the CMA, which can significantly alter the value of your home.

"Since it is my intent to focus my practice in this neighborhood, I'd be more than happy to take a look through your home to give you a quick valuation with absolutely no obligation on your part. It's just something I do with the hopes that if you did sell sometime in the future you might consider my services.

"You see, an appraiser would typically charge you around $500 to appraise your home, and I would do it at no charge to you.

"I also wouldn't want you to straighten up your home just for me. I'm a Realtor and we're very used to viewing homes before they're ready to show. I assure you it won't affect the value at all."

"Would this be of any benefit to you? "

(PAUSE – Let silence do the heavy lifting)

"Great! How about I swing by right after I lock-up here?"

Example of Back of Open House Flyer to Reference in Scripts

the CHARDONNAY MARKET UPDATE

A LOOK AT **YOUR** NEIGHBORHOOD

{10/1/2012 - PRESENT}

status	street	beds/baths	sq.footage	price
ACTIVE	W. Lakewood Dr.	4/3	3359	$620,000
ACTIVE	Lakewood Dr.	3/2.5	3042	$559,000
SOLD	Lakewood Ct.	4/4.5	3462	$530,000
SOLD	Chardonnay Ct.	4/3	3596	$565,000

Jillian Bos, "Visalia's Top Producing Luxury Specialist", is a graduate from Pepperdine University. Post graduation, she started her career in real estate at Sotheby's International Realty, specializing in the Brentwood, Westwood, Beverly Hills, and Santa Monica neighborhoods. After nine years in Southern California, Jillian moved "home" to Visalia.
Jillian is experienced in the art of guiding people through the experience of buying, selling, and investing in real estate. Jillian consistently earns accolades for her top sales performance. She is an expert negotiator, exhibits innovative marketing strategies and is dedicated to making the buying and selling process as enjoyable as possible.

THIS IS NOT INTENDED AS SOLICITATION IF YOUR HOME IS CURRENTLY REPRESENTED BY ANOTHER BROKER

search homes & connect with us @
WWW.JILLIANBOS.COM

[f] [P] [◎] [in] [≈] [8+] @JILLIANBOSDOTCOM

559.623.2195 | JILLIAN@KW.COM

kw | LUXURY HOMES INTERNATIONAL   400 EAST MAIN STREET | DOWNTOWN VISALIA

MODULE 15

ACTION STEPS:

1. **List the benefits:** Take a moment to outline your new Open House Strategy from now on. What will you focus on? List at least 3 items.

2. **Marketing and Promotion:** Create your blueprint for promoting events through as many means as you are able. Highlight where you'll need help, research, or systems.

3. **Practice your scripts:** From sellers to buyers, guests to vendors, your conversations are a big part of your promotion. You can start to get it right today with script and presentation practice. Imagine yourself in an Open House and being able to chat with every guest; collect all guests' contact information; even pre-sell a free valuation or listing. You can do it all – it is all in your preparation and prioritization. (See your responses to #1, "What will you focus on?")

In order to rapidly expand SOI Referral Databases, many top producing real estate agents are signing up with online review sources and search engines to generate more referrals.

Since 88% of home buyers initially search for a home on the internet (according to the National Association of REALTORS® Survey of Home Buyers & Sellers), it's important for real estate agents to appear prominently in the places where home buyers search for homes. With thousands of ads inviting us to 'click here', sophisticated and self-educating consumers are looking for real value. It is your job to provide it, and that means 'developing a web presence.'

That presence is multi-faceted – including your website and social media presence (Facebook and LinkedIn are the minimum), registration on review websites and directories, and local listing sites such as online Yellow Pages. But also list your company in online real estate directories of all types. This takes a bit of time, not much money, and preparation to develop.

In this module, we particularly address Review websites. In today's social media world, social proof – reviews and testimonials by real users of a company's products and services – is the #1 way people will decide to contact you (or to avoid doing so). Thus, you need to develop that channel of connecting with new faces.

As third-party review services and mobile apps have become the #1 must-read for any consumer to feel well educated in their choices, **your strategy for building an inventory of positive, detailed online reviews** is a vital component of your online presence.

How Consumers Are Searching

If your business has no professional-looking and professional-reading website today, you instantly lose credibility – and those potential business leads. Really, then, the first step in garnering online reviews is to create your own business website (along with your social media pages), fill it with easily and quickly readable content like FAQs (responses to frequently asked questions) and information about who you are, what you do and the services and areas of offer you have.

'Easy and quick' are the keys to writing up your web content. Short sentences. Images and graphics (a picture is worth a thousand words). Your picture.

This said, an online researcher who does not have your business name or know your own name will never find your site. **Online, being found by your target consumer is all about 'key words'.** It may be presumptuous to define what that means in our search-engine-driven world, but here is what it means:

Key words are single words, short phrases, or longer phrases both specifically and generically descriptive of your product or service.

*Key words you **must use** are those that the average consumers will choose to type into their Google, Yahoo or other search engine to find a specific service, business or product they seek.*

Who uses key words on the web? Everyone. Otherwise, you are on a dark, unlit stage, doing a silent mime act before an audience. No one sees you. No one finds you. Search engines, review websites, social media, personal, professional and company websites are all driven by key words.

Primary key words to consider for your (Memphis Tennessee) real estate business:

Real estate in Memphis
Full service real estate agent Memphis
Condos for sale Memphis
Free home appraisal Memphis

Up to you, but just go into your search engine now, and type 'real estate'. Results are in the millions and all over the map of the country. Your job is to load the content of your website with *specifics* that lead the search engine to your site every time.

Where Consumers Are Searching

Search Engines

Google, Yahoo pulls its ratings from Yelp, and Bing lacks a rating system, besides what rank a site will show up based on Search Engine Optimization.

Review Sites

Yelp, Angie's List, Yellow Pages.com, Glassdoor, Trip Advisor (with rentals), Realtor.com, Zillow, Hotpads. Each one has a menu link for businesses who wish to register.

Social Media

Facebook page reviews, Twitter, YouTube, Pinterest, LinkedIn

Your Web sites

Note that many professionals create both a personal/professional website and an agency/business website.

Other Sites

Blogs (integrated with or separate from your website), media/PR mentions, local publications or articles about you, contests you've been in and/or won, and annual rating awards.

Trust and Social Proof

Back to reviews. The most common way that consumers search for them is to type the keywords:

'ABC Realty Memphis Reviews'
'Bob Jones Realtor Reviews'

They will lead to all the review and other websites containing one or all of those key words – and for you, that is the goal! This is why many website and social media site owners don't call their client comments 'Testimonials' as often as 'Reviews' – almost no consumer Googles 'Bob Jones Realtor Testimonials'. 'Review' is the top key word.

What causes a review to be deemed trustworthy by consumers?

1. The content of the review – specific enough to know the writer really used the product/service

2. The number of reviews – shows that the business has a large following

3. A fair blend of good and bad reviews – no one believes or trusts you if you present only positive reviews

4. Star ratings – like Amazon's system, a positive written review can garner few stars because the writer is comparing your good service to other great ones

5. The website where the review is found – Yelp is among the best-known review site, but not all have great reputations

6. The credibility of the author who wrote the review – is the writer using the same level of language the consumer writes; if yes, that creates credibility

So, whether a client was elated with their purchase of a $3 million-dollar home after a 4-year process, or unhappy with an experience at an Open House and left after 5 minutes – you are likely to find the experience retold on one or more review sites.

Bad Reviews

Yelp has been accused – as have any number of business owners being reviewed on that site – of either front-loading bad reviews or trying to delete/censure them.

Here is the fact: You will get reviews that paint you as outstanding, good, mediocre, neutral and bad. Those reviewers will be painting you in glowing terms or ranting at their awful experience with you.

Angry clients, misunderstandings, bumpy transactions, or neglected follow-up could lead to a negative review, and therefore harm your business. Remember:

- Having a strategy for online reviews does not prevent a bad review.

- Good reviews, great reviews, and the benefits can far outweigh the bad ones over the long term. Stay the course.

- Learning is presented in many ways: Bad reviews can reveal to you some missed opportunities or pitfalls in your systems – so accept and correct them right away.

- The presence of a few bad reviews demonstrates that these are real reviews, not purchased, hyped or falsified content

- You may be able to bring a bad review to a happy ending, and display even better customer service to a new audience.

Listening to many actors and other celebrities on the subject, many say "I never read my reviews." True or not, **you must read reviews of your services and your business.** Respond to bad reviews by taking the 'high road' – politely, and in standard professional language, thanking the reviewer for his point of view and stating briefly how you will correct things in the future. Make such responses as soon as you can.

Create and Cast Your Net

Whether Zillow, Realtor.com, Yelp, or even on search engines like Google, Bing, and Yahoo, agents who appear often with good reviews garner more 'social proof' and are chosen much more frequently.

Much like your Multiple Listing Service, hundreds if not thousands of websites have widgets and algorithms that pull ratings and reviews from all types of sources. This casts a wider net for you.

Like any business plan, begin with a quick map of where you'd like to show up online. With each site you've identified, both where you're currently showing and where you'd like to start showing, look at how your clients go about submitting their referrals, and how you can check reviews on a regular basis. Each review site is a bit different.

Review sites may have their own rating system, settings where you can respond to consumer reviews, remove negative reviews (or be denied this option), or contact help desks for navigation, customization, reviewing sharing and syndication.

Put a weekly appointment for your staff to review these sites and flag the sites and the reviews that need your personal response.

Five-Star Reviews Can Generate Leads!

Transaction coordinator Courtney Downer, sharing how she includes client reviews in their transaction checklists for contract to close. **Take notes as you view this video:**

https://youtu.be/-r0CnHLAm2k

As explained in Courtney Downer's video interview, she generated 26 five-star Zillow reviews last year that collectively generate 25 to 30 leads a month.

Set Expectations from the Start

The process for obtaining five-star reviews starts at the initial buyer consultation or listing presentation. Have you seen that business whose '*20 Point Check System*' is mentioned so often, that the clients will start to use the phrase themselves? This is not an accidental 'key word choice' on the part of that business! It creates buzz. When that phrase is written or spoken, everyone knows who is being referenced.

Brand-building is 'keyed in' to 'key words'!

What are the key-word phrases that you can repeatedly use to *differentiate yourself from all other businesses.* Perhaps simply starting to say something like this to people in a consistent manner is all you need:

"Promise me that if anything is jeopardizing **your five-star** review that you'll tell me."
"Is there anything I can do to make it a **five-star experience** for you?"

Remind Throughout the Transaction

Continual reminders to clients about your five-star standards and goals for receiving great client reviews throughout transactions is essential. Use opportunities for providing good news to ask clients if they are receiving "five-star client review service" after a property appraises, an offer is accepted, and especially at closing.

Also know that by stating this high standard of customer service repeatedly to clients, agents are held accountable to ensure they deliver; make a promise, keep a promise.

At the end of each phase in your process, ask the clients what they've seen in their experiences with other businesses that you could do better.

"I want to thank you for your support this year. Can I ask a favor? What specifically about the newsletter do you look forward to? What are we missing that we can add?"

"Let's finish up today's showing with a review: What did you love about the houses we chose, and how could that be a 'plus' when showing you property in the future?"

"We've really had a focus on keeping our neighbors updated on this market we're in. What are some other practices you're learning from that we can adapt so that we bring you more value?"

Follow-up Questions as Prompts

The review sites provide a great framework for you and your reviewing clients. Most, by giving categories to select from, prompt the consumer to rate parts of your service, instead of your service as just one lump delivery – just as you did with the above questions you ask your clients at various stages of the transaction.

LinkedIn, for instance, asks about the type of expertise someone holds. Zillow asks how many stars you'd give for certain aspects of business. Amazon likes people to talk about delivery times as promised, no-hassle returns when they've been necessary, and the ability or not of the product to deliver on stated promises.

When a person tells you "I liked such-and-so about that restaurant", friends often ask a prompting question for more information: "What about the service – I heard it was slow?" etc. Likewise, you do this at different stages in your transactions and client interactions. "Did you like the Open House turnout?" is a wide-open leading question. As follow-up, you prompt, "What about the various questions people asked about the property – do you think they call for improvements before the next one?" or "How does this turnout compare to your prior expectations?"

Play to your strengths at each stage of your relationship, and you'll have a library of useable testimonials, reviews, suggestions and recommendations that will provide triggers for new clients to take action, and hire you. Ask your clients about:

- Your response time
- Your negotiation successes on client's behalf
- Your knowledge of the market
- Thoroughness of your customer service
- Anticipation by you of their needs
- Your respect of their time
- Your degree of organization
- Your consideration of their special needs and wants
- 5-Star moments they had

- The look and feel of your presentations and materials
- Technology you used
- Etc.

Then? **Ask if they would be so kind as to write that comment up on XYZ review website for you!** Like referrals, **the direct ask** is what gives you the most control and the best outcomes.

Ask for and Thank for Reviews

Yelp, Amazon, and Google collectively state that 50% or more of consumers take the time to review products and services of their own volition. If you seek a higher review percentage, remind clients and ask!

Thus as one way of creating a direct ask, at closing of the purchase or sale of their home, send a pre-templated email to all your clients with a **direct link to your review page of choice.** It is also a good idea to personalize the first and last few sentences of the email's text content for each client.

Include a copy/pasted reminder of each client's actual review in your SOI Database. That creates an immediate prompt for you to **thank the client for his gracious review the next time you make your scheduled phone contact with him.** It is also an opportunity to turn a personal email message to you from a client – or a comment he makes during a live conversation – into a review. **Ask, directly!**

"NAME, I am reviewing my notes, and your e-mail from Thursday read 'Tim, you really took the time to ask about our MUST haves, and what we could live without; this was so helpful!' Would you be okay with being a spokesperson by posting it here on this site?

"Would you mind taking a moment to copy/paste your gracious comments into a review website for me and my business? If you prefer, just authorize me to repost it myself – to save you time. Many thanks!

"**{LINK HERE}** Your comments will help other clients who've been where you were, to get to where you are now, and it helps us out, too! Thanks again."

Add a KPI for a 10% monthly increase in number of reviews this year!

Systemize a Successful Result

Just as you have systematically been asking for **referrals,** you must now start asking in a frequent and regular way for testimonials and online reviews. Add it to your scripts. Get comfortable recognizing a compliment when you hear it – then jump on the **direct ask for a review.**

Add client reviews to your website on a specifically-created page. Add them, as appropriate to their topic, to your flyers and mailers in a boxed section of a page. They might be one-liners, or whole essays! They might look like this:

ABC Realty saved us loads of money! They sent us to 3 of their Preferred Lenders and after interviewing them all, we got a loan for 1.25 points under what we expected. Thanks, Jack, for saving us all that money!

Thanks, Jack, for all your care. We love our new house!

Jack Roberts at ABC Realty helped us find our current home 3 years ago. Amazingly, he has kept in touch and when our son was looking for a condo, Jack was right there to guide him through the whole process. Painless! We trust Jack – he's like a member of the family.

1. **Get on Review Sites:** Create profiles on Zillow, Google, <u>realtor.com</u>, Yelp, and others that are attractive/known to you.

2. **Review Your Reviews:** Time-block a weekly review by your staff of posted testimonials and client reviews.

3. **Use Great Reviews:** Make sure staff knows to call your attention to bad reviews needing your personal online response. Make sure they collect and bring your awareness to particularly flattering reviews you will use in your flyers and mailings.

4. **Script It for Direct Asks:** Practice scripts, or just one-off questions to train clients to write reviews. You have the best results by directly asking for a review/testimonial – so do it.

Previewing property has been an effective method that many real estate agents have systematically implemented to get new listings while developing superior market knowledge. What isn't widely recognized is that this is also an extremely effective way to grow your SOI Referral Database quickly.

What is 'previewing property'? It is your knock-on-doors, feet-walking-the-neighborhood activity. You are equipped with flyers, CMA printouts, business cards. You will find that previewing property is one of the most cost-effective ways to rapidly grow a listing inventory with confidence when you are using these real estate scripts and techniques.

A confident attitude that you are performing an effective business-building activity must have been built into your knock-on-doors, too, however, so that you are not 'just going through the motions' or go about it as so much 'busy work'. People you encounter will know the difference!

How It Works

Agent Arthur started his business with property previewing. He always greeted each homeowner cheerfully and explained the value of the flyer he was delivering. On each successive visit after the first, he'd greet then ask the homeowner if he's heard of any neighbors looking to move – sell their home or buy elsewhere. He wrote the responses.

On successive visits, he found that a curious homeowner asked him to enter the house and property for 'a quick appraisal of market value.' He would then link up with his questions about if/how soon the owner was thinking about selling. Why move? Where to? And so on, developing the lead. Agent Arthur made sure he had complete contact information and, back at the office, entered the homeowner into his SOI Database and launched him on the Contact Plan.

Benefits of Previewing Property

By walking the neighborhood to preview properties, provide value through a flyer or answering real estate questions (general or specific), Agent Arthur came to give a growing number of 'quick appraisals' and over time gained many listings...as he grew his SOI Database. This last is the top benefit of previewing properties.

It's an extremely effective way:

1. for new agents without a large client database or name recognition to quickly gain immediate business

2. for all agents to continuously build and develop relationships for future business as you meet people in your neighborhoods of activity

3. for real estate agents that make previewing property a regular part of their schedule to develop a heightened understanding of the local inventory in their geographic area of activity.

After a period of time of previewing property, agents can respond confidently to questions in listing presentations about FSBOs, expired listings and other homes currently listed for sale. With buyers, agents can be adept at identifying options in available homes that maybe weren't shared during the pre-qualification process, or that their buyers realize are "must haves" as they walk through property. Additional benefits include:

- Collecting location details not indicated in marketing
- Seeing first-person the condition and features of a property
- Get listings for buyers who may not be listed on the multiple listing service (MLS) FSBOs
- Collect recently expired listings
- Develop your SOI Database with owners waiting to sell later, but valuing preparation that you offer
- Chatting with neighbors with their fingers on the pulse of the area

The level of confidence that an agent exudes after previewing property translates into instant local experience – trust – in the minds of prospective clients, because their representative took the extra step to verify what is marketed, saving the client time, and anticipating a customer care need or desire.

Top producing agent Brad Baldwin explains how he regularly previews properties to grow his massive listing inventory in this video. **Take notes as you view this video:**

Brad Baldwin

https://youtu.be/LYhqr14SfRY

How to Combine Previewing Property & Finding Listings

The process Brad Baldwin references begins by searching the MLS multiple listing service database for a group of 4 or 5 active listings located in a tight geographic area.

Then pull up the addresses of all the expired listings in the same area for the past 12 months before heading out to view the active listings you have scheduled. After you view each listing, knock on the doors of 2 houses to the left of the listing, 2 houses to the right, and 4-5 homes across the street. You can either use the map function from your Multiple listing service, request a plat map from your title agent, or pull a map like the one you see below from Google Maps, and create your target homes.

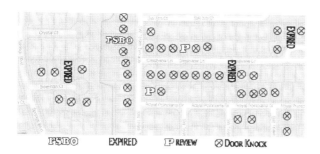

When knocking-on-doors, if you learn the owner's name, write this down as a reference point for the future and while talking with some of the other neighbors. As the neighborhood expert, how much more powerful is it to reference a neighbor's house as "Tom and Wendy's place, the blue home at 1917 Crescent" as opposed to "1917 Crescent Way"? You'll already know their address from door knocking; a handwritten note sent immediately afterwards could be a great touch to ease these folks into your SOI.

After a month of previewing property, you'll have created your own hyperlocal market research, complete with active, potential, and current off-the-market listings. Should a buyer ever ask what sets you apart from other agents, you have not only unparalleled market knowledge, you've got the proof to back it up.

To keep your **property previewing records** straight – and you must as this develops your SOI Database which in turn grows the number of referrals you will get – create a blank chart with headers on your spreadsheet software or other data tool (see image below). The headers make sure you capture the important information for the SOI Database, but make sure the information makes it into that Database the same day, and the Contact Plan is immediately launched for each new member.

Doing the Property Preview Math

While out previewing the **active listings**, be sure to knock on the doors of all the **expired listings** in the area. Also, be sure to contact all of the **For Sale by Owner listings** (FSBO) as well. For each one, knock on the doors of 2 houses to the left, 2 houses to the right, and 4 homes across the street using the same script provided in this module. The math shows that you will be making 8 door-knocks per listing.

Preview 8 listings in an afternoon, 8 doors knocked per listing, for a total of 64 doors.

5 active listings times 8 =	40 Doors Knocked
2 expired listings times 8 =	16 Doors Knocked
1 FSBO times 8 =	8 Doors Knocked
Total =	64 Doors

If you are able to knock on 64 doors, you will typically **speak to 25 or 30 people** you haven't met about their plans for moving and whether they know anyone looking to move soon. That is 25-30 individuals who have now heard your name and know what you do – a nice gain for a few hours walking. **3 days a week yields 75 new contacts** to begin to market to in an effort to become their real estate influencer of choice. If **just 5% buy or sell their homes with you**, that would be **864 opportunities, or 43.2 closed transactions.**

By scheduling Property Previewing regularly and recording information earned systematically, your database and referral business will start to increase rapidly, and so will the number of closed transaction and commissions.

One last reminder about Property Previewing: Every time you chat with an owner, you ask for referrals! What if we make a point to check back in with them in a week, since they may think of someone they didn't at the moment. Our calls-to-action can allow us to cast a wider net.

SCRIPT FOR DOOR KNOCKING AFTER PREVIEWING PROPERTY

Use this simple conversation with the 'investigative reporter' mindset to develop the most opportunity from each property you preview.

"Hi! I'm John Smith with ABC Realty, and we're trying to find a buyer for your neighbor's home, which has 4 bedrooms, 2 baths and is priced at $220,000. Who do you know who would like to move into the area?"

[Obtain the contact information of any lead they may give you, proceed with the script below]

"I ask because, as a neighbor, you have the best idea of who'd like to live here too" (Pause) "What caused you to choose this neighborhood?"   [Great, let me write that down]

"How long have you lived in this home?" [Repeat back to client]

"Where did you move from?" [Thank you for helping me!]

"Where would you move to – if you were going to move?"

"While we're here, when do you plan on moving?" [If they plan to move in less than a year, proceed with the script]

"Would it be of benefit to know what your home is currently worth and be able to start previewing homes online on your own?"

[Set an appointment to review comparison sales, set them up on a private MLS search, and list the property for sale]

[OR if they say, "We're not moving"]

Okay, great! I appreciate taking time with me today, would you do me a favor? Be on the lookout for some of our invitations! Thanks, again!

1. **Make It Worth It:** List 4 benefits to previewing properties for your current and future buyer clients, and 4 benefits for your current and future listing clients.

2. **Systematize:** Create a checklist for previewing property. What do you want to learn that would help grow your SOI Database, create a closed transaction for one of your buyers, earn referrals for listings, etc.?

3. **Map Your Previews:** Use the examples in this module to create your preview map, complete with area active listings, expired listings, and FSBO listings to make the most use of your knock-on-doors time. Target surrounding houses to multiply your door-knocking after previewing each property.

4. **Be Scripted:** Practice and finetune the provided scripts to help you obtain information from the homeowners in the surrounding homes, to find potential new listings and new SOI Database members.

5. **Do the Math:** Don't ever again go out to preview a single home. Map the neighborhood for FSBO, expired's, etc. and walk the neighborhood purposefully. Track your effectiveness. The Law of Great Numbers is on your side, creating results!

Made in the USA
Middletown, DE
11 January 2019